lonely planet

Fast Talk

Icelandic

Guaranteed to get you talking

Contents

≡ Special Features

5 **Phrases**
To Learn Before You Go... 6

10 **Phrases**
To Sound Like a Local 7

10 **Phrases**
To Start a Sentence........... 8

10 **Phrases**
To Get You Talking 88

Before You Go

Many visitors to Iceland get around without speaking a word of Icelandic, but just a few phrases go a long way in making friends, inviting service with a smile, and ensuring a rich and rewarding travel experience – you could discover a cosy thermal spring off the tourist track, experience a sublime meal, or grab that great shopping bargain.

Icelandic is a North Germanic language. Iceland was settled primarily by Norwegians in the 9th and 10th centuries. By the 14th century Icelandic (Old Norse) and Norwegian had grown apart considerably. This was due to changes in Norwegian, while Icelandic changed remarkably little through the centuries.

In fact, Iceland has an unbroken literary tradition, dating from about 1100. The treasures of the Sagas and the Poetic Edda, written about 700 years ago, can be enjoyed by a modern-day speaker of Icelandic.

Be aware, especially when you're trying to read bus timetables or road signs, that place names can be spelled in several different ways due to Icelandic grammar rules.

If you read our coloured pronunciation guides as if they were English, you'll be understood.

PRONUNCIATION TIPS

You'll find further pronunciation tips on p#, but to get you started:

★ The Icelandic alphabet consists of 32 letters: *a, á, b, d, e, é, f, g, h, i, í, j, k, l, m, n, o, ó, p, r, s, t, u, ú, v, x, y, ý, þ, ð, æ, ö.*

★ Double consonants are pronounced as such.

★ Stress is generally on the first syllable.

★ The Icelandic letter þ, represented as *th* in the pronunciation guide, is pronounced as the 'th' in 'thin', while ð, represented as *th*, is pronounced as the 'th' in 'lather'.

ARTHUR OR MARTHA?

When there are both feminine and masculine forms of a word, it's indicated in this book in either of two ways, with the feminine form always appearing first:

★ with a slash separating the feminine form and masculine ending (which is added to the feminine form) of a word:

hot   heit/-ur (f/m)
         hait/-oor

★ when the distinction between masculine and feminine is more complex, each word is given in full, separated with a slash:

cold   køld/kaldur (f/m)
         kerld/kuhld-oor

Fast Talk Icelandic

Don't worry if you've never learnt Icelandic (íslensku *ees-lehn-skö*) before – it's all about confidence. You don't need to memorise endless grammatical details or long lists of vocabulary – you just need to start speaking. You have nothing to lose and everything to gain when the locals hear you making an effort. And remember that body language and a sense of humour have a role to play in every culture.

"you just need to start speaking"

Even if you use the very basics, such as greetings and civilities, your travel experience will be the better for it. Once you start, you'll be amazed how many prompts you'll get to help you build on those first words. You'll hear people speaking, pick up sounds and expressions from the locals, see something on a billboard – all these things help to build your understanding.

5. Phrases to Learn Before You Go

1. Where's the next petrol station?
Hvar er næsta bensín stöð?

kvahrr ehrr nais-dah behn-seen sterth?

In the highlands you should check fuel levels and the distance to the next petrol station before setting off.

2. I'm looking for a public toilet.
Ég er að leita að almenningssalerni.

yehkh ehrr ahth lay-tah ahth ahl-mehn-inkhs-sahl-ehrr-dni

Major sights often have too few facilities for increasing visitor numbers; plan ahead and stop at facilities when you see them.

3. What would you recommend?
Hverju mælir þú með? kver·yu mai·lir thoo medh

Let a local recommend a delicious, fresh blast of local flavour.

4. I'd like a bottle of beer, please.
Get ég fengið bjór í flösku, takk.

get yekh fen·gidh byohr·ee fleusku tak

You must be at least 20 years old to buy alcohol, which is only sold in licensed bars, restaurants and government-run Vínbúðin liquor stores.

5. How do you say...?
Hvernig segir maður ...?

kvehrr-dnikh say-irr mahth-örr ...?

Most Icelanders speak English, but attempts to speak the local language will be much appreciated.

10. Phrases to Sound Like a Local

Cool!	**Kúl!**	kool
No worries.	**Engar áhyggiur.**	ayng-ahrr ow-higyrrö
Sure.	**Vissulega.**	viss-ö-lehkh-ah
No way!	**Ekki séns!**	ehky-i syens
Just joking!	**Bara grín!**	ba-rrah grreen
Too bad.	**En leitt.**	ehn layt
What a shame.	**En leiðinlegt.**	ehn layth-in-lehcht
What's up?	**Hvað segirðu (gott)?**	kvahth sagy-irr-th (gott)
Well done!	**Vel gert!**	vehl gyehrt
Not bad.	**Ekki slæmt**	ehky-i slaimt

10. Phrases to Start a Sentence

When is (the tour)?	Hvenær er (ferðin)?
	kveh-nahrr ehrr (fehrrth-in)

Where is (the bus stop)?	Hvar er biðstöðin?
	kvahrr ehrr bith-sterth-in?

Where can I (buy a ticket)?	Hvar get ég (keypt miða)?
	kvahrr geht yehkh (kayft mith-ah?)

Do you have (a map)?	Áttu (kort af staðnum)?
	owt-ö korrt ahv stahth-nöm?

Is there (a flight to...)?	Er (flogið til ...)?
	ehrr flo-yith til ...?

I'd like (a coffee).	Gæti ég fengið (kaffi).
	gyai-ti yehkh fayn-khith (kahf-fi)

I'd like to (return this).	Mig langar (að skila þessu).
	mikh lowng-ahr (ahth skhi-lah thehss).

Can I (take photographs)?	Má ég (taka myndir)?
	mow yehkh (tah-kah mind-irr)?

Do I need to (book)?	Þarf ég að (panta)?
	thahrrf yehkh ahth (pahn-tah)?

Can you (show me)?	Gætir þú (sýnt mér)?
	geh-törr thoo (seent myehrr)?

Chatting & Basics

≡ Fast Phrases

Hello./Goodbye.	Halló./Bless. hahl-loh/blehs
Please./Thank you.	Gjörðu svo vel./Takk fyrir. gyer-thö svo vehl/tahk firr-irr
Do you speak English?	Talar þú ensku? tah-lahrr <u>thoo</u> ehn-skö?

Essentials

Yes.	Já. yow
No.	Nei. nay
Please.	Gjörðu svo vel. gyer-thö svo vehl
Thank you.	Takk fyrir. tahk firr-irr
You're welcome.	Ekkert að þakka. ehk-ehrrt ahth <u>tha</u>hk-ah
Excuse me. (forgive me)	Afsakið. ahf-sahk-ith
Sorry.	Fyrirgefou. firr-irr-gyehv-thö

Fast Talk

Pronunciation

Below is a general pronunciation guide of Icelandic sounds, outlining in red our representation of each sound, used in the simplified transliterations throughout the book. Consonants not listed here are pronounced as in English.

Vowels

ah	as the 'a' in 'father'
uh	as the 'u' in 'cut'
a	as the 'a' in 'act'
eh	as the 'e' in 'bet'
ee	as the 'ee' in 'seethe'
i	as the 'i' in 'hit'
ü	a bit like the 'e' in British English 'dew' – try pursing your lips and saying 'ee'
o	a short 'o' as in 'pot'
oh	as the 'o' in 'note'
oo	a long 'oo' as in 'cool'
u	a short 'oo' as in 'foot'
ö	as the 'e' in 'summer'
or	as the 'or' in 'for', with less emphasis on the 'r'
er	as the 'er' in 'fern' but shorter, without the 'r'

Diphthongs

au	eör (there is no equivalent sound in English)
ae	as the 'ea' in 'bear'
ay	as the 'ay' in 'day'
ai	as the sound of 'eye'
oy	the 'oy' as in 'toy'
ow	as the 'ou' in 'out'

Semiconsonants

é	yeh (as in the 'ye' in 'yes')
w	as in 'wet'
y	as in 'yet'

Consonants

f	'f' as in English. When between vowels or at the end of a word it's pronounced as 'v'. When followed by l or n it's pronounced as 'b'.
g	'g' as the 'g' in 'get'; 'kh' between vowels or before r or ð, g has a guttural sound, as the 'ch' in Scottish 'loch'
h	'h' as in English, except when followed by v, when it's pronounced as 'k'
þ	represented as th; 'th' as the 'th' in 'thin'
ð	represented as th; 'th' as the 'th' in 'lather'
s	always as in 'kiss', never as in 'treasure'
sh	as in 'ship'
ch	as in 'chew'
dj	as the 'j' in 'jaw'
th	as the 'th' in 'lather'
ng	as in 'sing'
ngn	as the meeting of sounds in 'hang-nail'
rr	a trilled 'r'
rt	as the 'rt' in American English 'start'
rd	as the 'rd' in American English 'weird'
rn	as the 'rn' in American English 'earn'
rl	as the 'rl' in American English 'earl'
dn	as the 'dn' in 'hadn't'
dl	as the 'dl' in 'saddle'

Fast Talk

Names

Icelanders use the ancient patronymic system, where son, 'son' or dóttir, 'daughter' is attached to the genitive form of the father's or, less commonly, the mother's, first name. The telephone book entries are listed according to first names.

Language Difficulties

Do you speak English?	Talar þú ensku? tah-lahrr thoo ehn-skö?
Does anyone speak English?	Talar einhver ensku? tah-lahrr ayn-kvehrr ehn-skö?
I understand.	Ég skil. yehkh skil
I don't understand.	Ég skil (ekki). yehkh skil (ehk-i)
I speak a little Icelandic.	Ég tala svolitla íslensku. yehkh tah-lah svoh lit-lah ees-lehn-skö
What does ... mean?	Hvað þýðir ...? kvahth theeth-irr?
How do you say...?	Hvernig segir maður ...? kvehrr-dnikh say-irr mahth-örr ...?
Could you repeat that?	Gætir þú endurtekið þetta? gyai-tirr thoo ehn-dörr-tehk-ith theht-ah?

Could you please speak more slowly?	Gætir þú talað svolítið hægar? gyai-tirr <u>thoo</u> tah-lahth svo-lee-tith haikh-ahrr?

Greetings

Hello.	Halló. hahl-loh
Good morning/afternoon.	Góðan daginn. gohth-ahn dai-in
Good evening/night.	Gott kvöld./Góða nótt. khot kverld/khoh-th-ah noht
Goodbye.	Bless. blehs
How are you?	Hvernig hefur þú það? kvehrr-dnikh heh-vörr <u>thoo</u> <u>thath</u>?
Well, thanks.	Gott, takk. khot tahk

Titles

Sir/Mr	herra hehrr-rrah
Madam/Mrs	frú frroo
Miss	ungfrú oong-frroo

Fast Talk Titles
Icelanders are a rather informal people. A person is very rarely addressed by title and/or surname.

Introductions

What's your name?	Hvað heitir þú? kvahth hay-tirr-<u>thoo</u>?
My name is ...	Ég heiti ... yehkh hay-ti ...
I'm pleased to meet you.	Komdu sæl/sæll. (f/m) kon-dö sail/saidl

Personal Details

Where are you from?	Hvaðan ert þú? kvahth-ahn ehrrt <u>thoo</u>?

PHRASE BUILDER

I'm from ...	Ég er frá ...	yehkh ehrr frrow ...
Australia	Ástralíu	owst-rrah-lee-ö
Canada	Kanada	kaha-nah-dah
England	Englandi	aynkh-lahn-di
Ireland	Írlandi	eer-lahn-di
Scotland	Skotlandi	skot-lahn-di
the USA	Bandaríkjunum	bahnd-ah-rree-kyö-nöm

Family

Are you married?	Ert þú gift/giftur? (f/m)	ehrrt-ö gift/gift-örr?
I'm single.	Ég er einhleyp/einhleypur. (f/m)	yehkh ehrr ayn-hlayp/ayn-hlayp-örr
I'm married.	Ég er gift/giftur. (f/m)	yehkh ehrr gift/gift-örr

| Do you have a boyfriend/ girlfriend? | Átt þú kærasta/ kærustu? | owt <u>thoo</u> kairr-ahs-dah/ kairr-ös-dö? |

Age

| How old are you? | Hvað ertu gömul/gamall? (f/m) kvahth ehrr-dö gör-möl/gahm-ahdl? |
| I'm ... years old. | Ég er ... ára. yehkh ehrr ... ow-rrah |

Occupations & Study

| What do you do? | Hvað gerir þú? kvahth gehrr-irr <u>thoo</u>? |
| I'm an office worker. | Ég er skrifstofumaður yehkh ehrr skrrif-stof-ö-mahth-örr |

PHRASE BUILDER

I'm (a/an) ...	Ég er ...	yehkh ehrr ...
scientist	vísindamaður	vee-sin-dah-mahth-örr
student	námsmaður	nowms-mahth-örr
teacher	kennari	kehn-ah-rri
journalist	fréttamaður	frryeht-ah-mahth-örr
nurse	hjúkrunar- fræðingur	hyook-rrön-ahrr- frraith-ing-örr
waiter	þjónn/þjónus- tustúlka	thyohdn/thyohn-ös- dö-stool-kah

15

Relgion

What is your religion?	Hverrar trúar ert þú? kvehrr-ahrr trroo-ahrr ehrrt thoo?
I'm not religious.	Ég er ekki trúuð/ trúaður. (f/m) yehkh ehr ehk-i trroo-öth/ trroo-ahth-örr

PHRASE BUILDER

I'm ...	Ég er ...	yehkh ehrr ...
Buddhist	búddatrúar	boo-dah-trroo-ahrr
Catholic	kaþólsk/ kaþól-skur (f/m)	kah-tholsk/kah-thol-skörr
Christian	kristinnar trúar	krrist-in-ahrr trroo-ahrr
Hindu	hindú trúar	hin-doo trroo-ahrr
Jewish	gyðingur	gith-ing-örr
Muslim	múhameðs-trúar	moo-hah-mehths-trroo-ahrr

Feelings

I'm (cold/hot).	Mér er kalt/heitt. myehrr ehrr kahlt/hayt
I'm worried.	Ég hef áhyggjur. yehkh hehf ow-hig-yörr
I'm sorry. (condolence)	Mér þykir það leitt. myehrr thik-irr thahth layht
I (don't) like ...	Ég er (ekki) hrifinn af ... yehkh ehrr (ehk-i) hrri-vin ahv

PHRASE BUILDER

I'm...	Ég er ...	yehkh ehrr ...
angry	reið/reiður (f/m)	rrayth/rrayth-örr
grateful	þakklát/ þakklátur (f/m)	thahk-lowt/ thahk-law-törr
happy	glöð/ glaður (f/m)	glerth/ glah-thörr
hungry	svöng/ svangur (f/m)	sveörnkh/ svown-görr
sad	hrygg/hryggur (f/m)	hrrig/hrrig-görr
tired	þreytt/þreyttur (f/m)	thrrayt/thrrayt-örr
well	frísk/frískur (f/m)	frreesk/frrees-görr

Numbers

0	núll	nool
1	einn	aydn
2	tveir	tvayrr
3	þrír	<u>th</u>rreer
4	fjórir	fyoh-rrirr
5	fimm	fimm
6	sex	sehks
7	sjö	syer
8	átta	owt-dah
9	níu	nee-ö
10	tíu	tee-ö
20	tuttugu	tö-tökh-ö
21	tuttugu og einn	tö-tö-gö og aydn

17

30	þrjátíu	thrryow-tee-ö
40	fjörutíu	fyer-tee-ö
50	fimmtíu	fim-tee-ö
60	sextíu	sehks-tee-ö
70	sjötíu	syer-tee-ö
80	áttatíu	ow-tah-tee-ö
90	níutíu	nee-tee-ö
100	eitt hundrað	ayt hön-drraht
1000	eitt þúsund	ayt thoos-önd
one million	ein milljón	ayn mil-yohn

Time

What date is it today?	Hvaða dagur er í dag?
	kvahth-ah dahkh-örr ehrr ee dahkh?
What time is it?	Hvað er klukkan?
	kvahth ehrr klök-ahn?
It's ... am/pm.	Hún er ... fyrir hádegi/ eftir hádegi.
	hoon ehrr ... firr-irr how-day-i/ ehf-dirr how-day-i
in the morning	að morgni
	ahth mo-dni
in the evening	að kvöldi
	ahth kverl-di

Days

Monday	mánudagur	mow-nö-dahkh-örr
Tuesday	þriðjudagur	thrrith-yö-dahkh-örr
Wednesday	miðvikudagur	mith-vik-ö-dahkh-örr

Fast Talk Neologisms

The practice of creating neologisms (new words) instead of adopting foreign words is well established in Iceland. Neologisms such as útvarp, 'radio', sjónvarp, 'television', tölva, 'computer', and þota, 'jet', are just a few that have become part of the Icelandic vocabulary in the last 50 years.

Thursday	fimmtudagur	fim-tö-dahkh-örr
Friday	föstudagur	fers-dö-dahkh-örr
Saturday	laugardagur	leörkh-ah-dahkh-örr
Sunday	sunnudagur	sön-ö-dahkh-örr

Months

January	janúar	yah-noo-ahrr
February	febrúar	fehb-rroo-ahrr
March	mars	mahrrs
April	apríl	ah-prreel
May	maí	mai
June	júní	yoo-nee
July	júlí	yoo-lee
August	ágúst	ow-goost
September	september	sehft-ehm-behrr
October	október	okt-oh-behrr
November	nóvember	noh-vehm-behrr
December	desember	dehs-ehm-behrr

19

Dates

today	í dag ee dahkh
this morning	í morgun ee morr-gön
tonight	í kvöld ee kverld
this week	í þessari viku ee thehs-ahrri vi-kö
this year	á þessu ári ow thehs-ö owrr-i
now	núna noo-nah

Weather

What's the weather like?	Hvernig er veðrið? kvehrr-dnikh ehrr vehth-rrith?
It's ... today.	Það er ... í dag. tha-th ehrr...ee dahkh

PHRASE BUILDER

Will it be ... tomorrow?	Verður ... á morgun?	vehrrth-örr ... ow morr-khön?
cloudy	skýjað	skee-yahth
cold	kalt	kahlt
hot	heitt	hayt
raining	rigning	rrikh-neenkh
snowing	snjór	snyohrr
sunny	sólskin	sohl-skin
windy	hvasst	kvahst

Directions

Where is ...?	Hvar er ...?
	kvahrr ehrr ...?
How do I get to ...?	Hvernig kemst ég til ...?
	kvehrr-dnikh kyehmst yehkh til ...?
Is it far from here?	Er það langt héðan?
	ehrr <u>tha</u>th lowngt hyehth-ahn?
Can I walk there?	Er það í göngufæri?
	ehrr <u>tha</u>th ee gern-gö fai-rri?

PHRASE BUILDER

Turn left/ right at the ...	Beygðu til vinstri/ hægri við ...	baykh-thö til vinst-rri/ haikh-rri vith ...
next corner	næsta horn	nais-dah horrdn
traffic lights	umferðarljósin	öm-fehrrth-ahrr-ljohs-in

behind	fyrir aftan
	firr-irr ahft-ahn
in front of	fyrir framan
	firr-irr frrahm-ahn
far	langt í burtu
	lownkht ee börr-dö
near	nálægt
	now-laikht
opposite	á móti
	ow moh-ti

Airport & Transport

≡ Fast Phrases

When's the next bus?	Hvenær kemur næsti vagn? kveh-nairr kehm-örr naist-i vahgn?
Which bus goes to ...?	Hvaða rúta fer til ...? kvahth-ah roo-ta fehrr til ...?
I'd like a one-way ticket.	Gæti ég fengið miða/báðar leiðir? gyai-ti yehkh fayn-khith mith-ah/ahth-rrah layth-in-ah?

At the Airport

Is there a flight to ...?	Er flogið til ...? ehrr flo-yith til ...?
How long does the flight take?	Hvað er þetta langt flug? kvahth ehrr <u>theh</u>-tah lowngt flüg?

PHRASE BUILDER

At what time does the ... leave?	Hvenær fer/ kemur ...?	kveh-nayrr fehrr/ keh-mörr ...?
aeroplane	flugvélin	flökh-vyehl-in
boat	báturinn	bow-törr-in
(city)bus	strætó	strai-toh

22

BROTTFÖR	DEPARTURES
KOMA	ARRIVALS
MIÐASALA	TICKET OFFICE
STRÆTISVAGNABIÐSTÖÐ	BUS STOP
STÖÐ	STATION
TÍMAÁÆTLUN	TIMETABLE

airport tax	flükhvallaskattur
	flükh-vadla-skah-türr
boarding pass	brottfararspjald
	brroht-fah-rrahrr-spyald

Buying Tickets

Where can I buy a ticket?	Hvar get ég keypt miða?
	kvahrr geht yehkh kayft mith-ah?
I want to go to ...	Ég vil fara til ...
	yehkh vil fah-rrah til ...
Do I need to book?	Þarf ég að panta?
	thahrrf yehkh ahth pahn-tah?
I'd like to book a seat to ...	Gæti ég pantað far til ...
	gyai-ti yehkh pahn-tahth fahrr til ...
Is it completely full?	Er alveg fullt?
	ehrr ahl-vehkh fölt?
Can I get a stand-by ticket?	Get ég fengið forfallamiða?
	gyeht yehkh fayn-gith forr-fahd-lah-mith-ah?
Can I have a refund?	Gæti ég fengið endurgreiðslu?
	gyai-ti yehkh fayn-gith ehnd-örr-grrayths-lö?

AIRPORT & TRANSPORT

23

PHRASE BUILDER

I'd like ...	Gæti ég fengið ...	gyai-ti yehkh fayn-khith ...
a one-way ticket	miða/aðra leiðina	mith-ah/ahth-rrah layth-in-ah
a return ticket	miða/báðar leiðir	mith-ah/bowth-ahrr layth-irr
two tickets	tvo miða	tvo mith-ah
a student's fare	námsmanna-miða	nowms-mahn ah-mith-ah
1st class	fyrsta farrými	firrst-ah fahrr-rreem-i
2nd class	annað farrými	ahn-ahth fahrr-rreem-i

Bus

Where is the bus stop?	Hvar er biðstöðin? kvahrr ehrr bith-sterth-in?
Which bus goes to ...?	Hvaða vagn fer til ...? kvahth-ah vahkhn fehrr til ...?
Could you let me know when we get to ...?	Gætir þú látið mig vita þegar við komum til ...? gyai-tirr thoo low-tith mikh vi-tah thehkh-ahrr vith kom-öm til ...?
I want to get off!	Ég vil fara út! yehkh vil fah-rrah oot!

PHRASE BUILDER

What time is the ... bus?	Hvenær kemur ... strætó?	kveh-nairr kehm-örr ... strai-toh?
first	fyrst	firrst
next	næst	naist
last	síðast	seeth-ahst

Local Knowledge

Where is the train station?

There are no trains in Iceland, but there are plenty of buses!

Taxi

Please take me to ...	Gætir þú ekið mér til ...? gyai-tir <u>thoo</u> ehkith myehrr til ...?
How much does it cost to go to ...?	Hvað kostar að fara til ...? kvahth kost-ahrr ahth fah-rrah til ...?
Here is fine, thank you.	Hérna er ágætt, takk. hyehrr-dnah ehrr ow-gyait tahk
The next street to the left/right.	Næsta gata til vinstri/hægri. nais-tah gah-tah til vinst-rri/haikh-rri
Continue.	Haltu áfram. hahl-dö ow-frrahm
Stop here!	Stansa hérna! stahn-sah hyehrr-dnah!

Car & Motorbike

Where's the next petrol station?	Hvar er næsta bensín stöð? kvahrr ehrr nais-dah behn-seen-sterth?
The battery is flat.	Geymirinn er rafmagnslaus. gaym-irr-in ehrr rahv-mahgns-leös
The radiator is leaking.	Vatnskassinn lekur. vahs-kahs-in leh-körr
I have a flat tyre.	Það er sprungið hjá mér. <u>thahth</u> ehrr sprroon-ghith hyow myer

25

Local Knowledge

The Ring Road

Route 1 (Þjóðvegur 1), known as the Ring Road, is the country's main thoroughfare, comprising a super-scenic 1330km (830 miles) of mostly paved highway. It's rarely more than one lane in either direction. Countless gems line its path, while secondary roads lead off it to further-flung adventures.

It's overheating.	Hann hefur ofhitnað.	
	hahn heh-vör of-hit-nath	
It's not working.	Hann virkar ekki.	
	hahn virrk-ahrr ehk-i	
air (for tyres)	loft (í dekk)	
	loft (ee dehk)	
battery	rafgeymir	
	rrahf-gay-mirr	
brakes	bremsur	
	brrehm-sörr	

🔍 LOOK FOR

ALLUR AKSTUR BANNAÐUR	NO ENTRY
BIÐSKYLDA	GIVE WAY
BLÝLAUST	UNLEADED
EÐLILEGT	NORMAL
EINSTEFNA	ONE WAY
ENGIN BÍLASTÆÐI	NO PARKING
SJÁLFSAFGREIÐSLA	SELF SERVICE
STANS	STOP
SUPER	SUPER
VERKSTÆÐI	GARAGE
VÉLVIRKI	MECHANIC
VIÐGERÐIR	REPAIRS

clutch	kúpling koop-leeng
driver's licence	ökuskírteini ehr-kö-skeer-tay-ni
engine	vél vyehl
lights	ljós lyohs
radiator	vatnskassi vahss-kahss-i
road map	vegakort vehkh-ah-korrt
tyres	dekk dehk
windscreen	framrúða frrahm-rrooth-ah

Accommodation

≡ Fast Phrases

Do you have any rooms available?	Eru einhver herbergi laus? ehrr-ö ayn-kvehrr hehrr-behrr-khi leörs?
We're leaving now/tomorrow.	Við erum að fara núna/á morgun. vith ehrr-öm ahth fah-rrah noo-nah/ow morr-goon
I'd like to pay the bill.	Ég vil borga reikninginn. yehkh vil borr-khah rraykn-inkh-in

Finding Accommodation

PHRASE BUILDER

Where's a ...hotel?	Hvar er ... hótel?	kvahrr ehrr ... ho-tehl?
cheap	ódýrt	oh-deert
nearby	nálægt	now-laikht
clean	hreint	hrraynt

 **LOOK FOR**

FARFUGLAHEIMILI	YOUTH HOSTEL
GISTIHEIMILI	GUESTHOUSE
GISTIHÚS	MOTEL
HÓTEL	HOTEL
TJALDSTÆÐI	CAMPING GROUND

Booking & Checking In

What is the address?	Hvað er heimilisfangið? kvahth ehrr hay-mil-is-fown-gith?
Could you write the address, please?	Gætir þú skrifað niður heimilisfangið? gyai-tirr <u>thoo</u> skrrif-ahth nith-örr hay-mil-is fown-gith?
Do you have any rooms available?	Eru einhver herbergi laus? ehrr-ö ayn-kvehrr hehrr-behrr-khi leörs?
How many nights?	Hvað margar nætur? kvahth mahrr-gahrr nai-törr?
How much is it per night/per person?	Hvað kostar nóttin fyrir manninn? kvahth kost-ahrr noht-in firr-irr mahn-in?

◀)) **LISTEN FOR**

Sorry, we're full.	Mér þykir það leitt, en það er fullbókað. myehrr <u>thi</u>-kirr <u>thath</u> layt ehn <u>thath</u> ehrr födl boh-kahth

PHRASE BUILDER

I'd like ...	Gæti ég fengið ...	gyai-ti yehkh fayn-khith ...
a single room	einstaklings- herbergi	ayn-stahk-lings- hehrr-behrr-khi
a double room	tveggjamanna- herbergi	tvehg-yah-mahn-ah hehrr-behrr-gi
a room with a bathroom	herbergi með baði	hehrr-behrr-khi mehth bahht-i
to share a dorm	að deila herbergi með öðrum	ahth day-lah hehrr-behrr-khi mehth erth-rröm
a bed	rúm	rroom

I'm going to stay for ...	Ég verð ... yehkh vehrrth ...
one day	einn dag aydn dahkh
two days	tvo daga tvo dahkh-ah
one week	eina viku ay-nah vi-kö

Requests

Can I see it?	Má ég sjá það? mow yehkh syow thahth?
Are there any other/ cheaper rooms?	Eru nokkur önnur/ ódýrari herbergi? eh-rrö nok-örr ern-örr/ oh-deer-ah-rri hehrr-behrr-gi?

Is there a reduction for students/children?	Er afsláttur fyrir námsmenn/börn?
	ehrr ahf-slowt-örr firr-irr nowms-mehn/berdn?
Does it include breakfast?	Er morgunmatur innifalinn?
	ehrr morrkh-ön-maht-örr in-i-fahl-in?
It's fine, I'll take it.	Það er ágætt, ég fæ það.
	thahth ehrr ow-gyait yehkh fai thahth
I'm not sure how long I'm staying.	Ég er ekki viss um hvað ég verð lengi.
	yehkh ehrr ehk-i viss öm kvahth yehkh vehrrth layn-gi
Where is the bathroom?	Hvar er baðherbergið?
	kvahrr ehrr bahth-hehrr-behrr-gith?
May I leave these in your safe?	Má ég geyma þetta í öryggishólfi?
	mow yehkh gay-mah theh-dah ee er-ikh-is-hohl-vi?
Is there somewhere to wash clothes?	Er einhversstaðar hægt að þvo þvott?
	ehrr ayn-kvehrrs-stahth-ahrr haikht ahth thvo thvoht?
Can I use the kitchen?	Má ég nota eldhúsið?
	mow yehkh no-tah ehld-hoos-ith?
Can I use the telephone?	Má ég nota símann?
	mow yehkh no-tah see-mahn?

Camping

Am I allowed to camp here?	Má ég tjalda hér?
	mow yehkh tyahl-dah hyehrr?
Is there a campsite nearby?	Er tjaldstæði hér nálægt?
	ehrr tyahld-staith-i hyehrr now-laikht?

Useful Words - Accommodation

bathroom	baðherbergi	bahth-hehrr-behrr-gi
bed	rúm	rroom
blanket	teppi	teh-bi
clean	hreinn	hrraydn
dirty	óhreinn	ow-hrraydn
double bed	tvíbreitt rúm	tvee-brrayt rroom
electricity	rafmagn	rrahv-mahgn
excluded	fyrir utan	firr-irr öt-ahn
fan	vifta	vif-dah
included	innifalið	in-i-fahl-ith
key	lykill	li-kidl
lift (elevator)	lyfta	lif-dah
light bulb	ljósapera	lyow-sah-peh-rrah
a lock	lás	lows
mirror	spegill	spay-idl
pillow	koddi	kod-di
quiet	hljótt	hlyoht
sheet	lak	lahk
shower	sturta	störr-dah
soap	sápa	sow-pah
toilet	klósett/ salerni	kloh-seht/ sahl-ehrr-dni
toilet paper	klósettpappír	klow-seht-pah-peer
towel	handklæði	hahnd-klai-thi
(cold/hot) water	(kalt/heitt) vatn	(kahlt/hayt) vahtn
window	gluggi	khlö-khi

Local Knowledge Camping

When camping in parks and reserves the usual rules apply: leave sites as you find them; use biodegradable soaps; and carry out your rubbish.

Campfires are not allowed, so bring a stove. Butane cartridges and petroleum fuels are available in petrol stations. Blue Campingaz cartridges are not always readily available; the grey Coleman cartridges are more common.

Most campsites open mid-May to mid-September. Large campsites that also offer huts or cottages may be open year-round. This is a fluid situation, as an increasing number of visitors are hiring campervans in the cooler months and looking to camp with facilities – ask at local tourist offices for info and advice.

If camping in summer, be aware that if the weather turns bad and you'd like to sleep with a roof over your head, you'll be extremely lucky to find last-minute availability in guesthouses or hostels.

Useful Words - Camping

backpack	bakpoki	bahk-po-ki
can opener	dósaopnari	doh-sah-op-nah-rri
firewood	eldiviður	ehld-i-vith-örr
gas cartridge	gaskútur	gahs-koo-törr
mattress	dýna	dee-nah
penknife	vasahnífur	vah-sah-hneev-örr
rope	snæri	snai-rri
tent (pegs)	tjald(hælar)	tyahld(-hai-lahrr)
torch/flashlight	vasaljós	vah-sah-lyohs
sleeping bag	svefnpoki	svehbn-po-ki
stove	eldavél	ehld-ah-veel
water bottle	vatnsflaska	vahs-flahs-ga

Eating & Drinking

Fast Phrases

Can I see the menu, please?	Get ég fengið að sjá matseðilinn? gyeht-yehkh fayn-gith ahth syow maht-sehth-il-in?
I'd like a (bottle of beer), please.	Get ég fengið (bjór í flösku), takk. get yekh fen·gidh (byohrr ee·flersk-ö) tak

Meals

breakfast	morgunmatur morr-gön-mah-törr
lunch	hádegismatur how-day-is-maht-örr
dinner	kvöldmatur kverld-maht-örr

Fast Talk Alcohol

Alcohol was prohibited in Iceland in 1912. Beer wasn't legalised again until 1 March 1989, now known as Bjórdagurinn, 'beer day'.

Ordering & Paying

Can I see the menu, please?	Get ég fengið að sjá matseðilinn?
	gyeht-yehkh fayn-gith ahth syow maht-sehth-il-in?
What does it include?	Hvað er innifalið?
	kvahth ehrr in-i-fahl-ith?
Is service included in the bill?	Er þjónusta innifalin?
	ehrr thyoh-nös-dah in-i-fahl-in?
I'll have a ...	Ég ætla að fá ...
	yekh ait-lahth fow ...
✂ Cheers!	Skál!
	skowl

PHRASE BUILDER

I'd like a/the ..., please.	Get ég fengið ..., takk.	get yekh fen·gidh ... tak
table for (four)	borð fyrir (fjóra)	bordh fi·rir (fyoh·ra)
bill	reikninginn	rayk·nin·gin
drink list	vínseðillinn	veen·se·dhit·lin
menu	matseðillinn	mat·se·dhit·lin
that dish	þennan rétt	the·nan rryeht
bottle of (beer)	(bjór í) flösku	(byohr ee)·flersk·ö
(cup of) coffee/ tea	kaffi /te (bolla)	kah·fi /te (bo·dlah)
glass of (wine)	(vín)glas	(veen)·glas
water	vatn	vahtn

35

Fast Talk

Practising Icelandic

If you want to practise your language skills, try the waiters at a restaurant. Find your feet with straightforward phrases such as asking for a table and ordering a drink, then initiate a conversation by asking for menu recommendations or asking how a dish is cooked. And as you'll often know food terms even before you've 'officially' learnt a word of the language, you're already halfway to understanding the response.

Utensils

ashtray	öskubakki	ers-kö-bah-khi
a cup	bolli	bod-li
a drink	drykkur	drrik-örr
a fork	gaffall	khahf-adl
a glass	glas	khlahs
a knife	hnífur	hnee-vörr
a plate	diskur	disk-örr
a spoon	skeið	skayth
teaspoon	teskeið	teh-skayth

Special Diets & Allergies

I'm a vegetarian.	Ég er grænmetisæta.
	yehkh ehrr grrain-meht-is-ai-tah
I don't eat meat.	Ég borða ekki kjöt.
	yehkh borr-thah ehk-i kyert
Do you have vegetarian food?	Erud þið með grænmetisrétti?
	ehrr-öth <u>th</u>ith mehth grain·me·tis·rye·ti

Staple Foods & Condiments

bread	brauð	brreörth
cream	rjómi	rryoh-mi
eggs	egg	ehg
fish	fiskur	fis-körr
fruit	ávextir	ow-vehg-stirr
ketchup	tómatsósa	toh-mahts-soh-sah
meat	kjöt	kyert
mustard	sinnep	sin-nehp
pepper	pipar	pi-pahrr
potatoes	kartöflur	kahrr-ter-blörr
rice	hrísgrjón	hrrees-grryohn
salt	salt	sahlt
sauce	sósa	soh-sah
seasoning	krydd	krridd
sugar	sykur	si-görr
vegetables	grænmeti	grrain-meh-ti

Local Knowledge

Icelandic Cuisine

If people know anything about Icelandic food, it's usually to do with a plucky population tucking into boundary-pushing dishes such as fermented shark or sheep's head. So it's a delight to discover the more palatable options offered up by Iceland's delicious, fresh-from-the-farm ingredients, the seafood bounty hauled from the surrounding icy waters, the innovative dairy products (hello, skyr!) and the clever, historic food-preserving techniques that are finding new favour with today's much-feted New Nordic chefs.

Breakfast Menu

boiled egg	soðið egg	so-thith ehg
bread	brauð	brreörth
bread roll	rúnstykki	rroon-stih-kyi
butter	smjör	smyeörrr
cereal	morgun-korn	morr-gön-korrdn
cheese	ostur	ostörr
coffee	kaffi	kahf-fi
fruit juice	ávaxta-safi	ow-vah-tah-sah-vi
honey	hunang	hö-nowng
jam	sulta	söl-tah
marmalade	marme-laði	mahrr-meh-lah-thi
milk	mjólk	myohlk
muesli	múslí	moos-dlee
oatmeal	hafra-grautur	hahv-rrah-grreör-törr

Local Knowledge

Food Heritage

For much of its history, Iceland was a poverty-stricken hinterland. Sparse soil and cursed weather produced limited crops, and Icelandic farmer-fishers relied heavily on sheep, fish and seabirds to keep them from starving. Every part of every creature was eaten – fresh or dried, salted, smoked, pickled in whey or even buried underground (in the case of shark meat), with preserving techniques honed to ensure food lasted through lean times.

Local food producers and chefs today are rediscovering old recipes and techniques with a renewed sense of pride in the country's culinary heritage, and the results can be quite special. The strong Slow Food Movement prioritises locally grown food over imports, with restaurants proudly flagging up regional treats.

orange juice	appelsínnsafi	ah-pehl-see-nö-sah-vi
sour milk (type of yoghurt)	súrmjólk	soorr-myohlk
sugar	sykur	si-görr
tea	te	teh
toast	ristað brauð	rris-tahth brreötth
yoghurt	jógúrt	yoh-goorrt

Meat & Poultry

beef	nautakjöt	neör-tah-kyert
chicken	kjúklingur	kyoohk-leen-görr
ham	skinka	skin-kah
lamb	lambakjöt	lahm-bah-kyert
pork	svínakjöt	svee-nah-kyert
reindeer	hreindýrakjöt	hrrayn-dee-rrah-kyert
sausage	pylsa	pil-sah
turkey	kalkúnn	kahl-koodn

Fish

cod	þorskur	thorrsk-örr
haddock	ýsa	ee-sah
halibut	lúða	loo-thah
herring	síld	seeld
lobster	humar	hö-mahrr
(smoked) salmon	(reyktur) lax	(rraykh-dörr) lahks
scallop	hörpudiskur	her-rr-pö-dis-körr
shrimp	rækja	rrai-kyah

Fruit

apples	epli	ehb-li
apricots	apríkósur	ah-prree-koh-sörr
bananas	bananar	bah-nah-nahrr
blueberries	bláber	blow-behrr
crowberries	krækiber	krrai-kyi-behrr
grapes	vínber	veen-behrr
lemon	sítróna	see-trroh-nah
oranges	appelsínur	ah-pehl-see-nörr
peaches	ferskjur	fehrrs-kyörr
pears	perur	peh-rrörr
pineapple	ananas	ah-nah-nahs
strawberries	jarðar-ber	yahrr-thahrr-behrr

Vegetables

cabbage	hvítkál	kveet-kowl
carrots	gulrætur	göl-rrai-törr
cauliflower	blómkál	blohm-kowl
cucumber	gúrka	goorr-kah
garlic	hvítlaukur	kveet-leör-körr
green peas	grænar baunir	grrai-nahrr beör-nirr
green pepper	græn paprika	grrain pah-prri-kah
lettuce	salat	sah-lahd
mushrooms	sveppir	sveh-pirr
onion	laukur	leör-körr
potatoes	kartöflur	kahrr-ter-blörr

Desserts

biscuits	smákökur/kex	smow-ker-körr/kehgs
cake	kaka	kahkah
fruit	ávextir	ow-vehgs-tirr
ice cream	ís/rjómaís	ees/rryoh-mah-ees
pancakes	pönnukökur	per-nö-ker-körr
pudding	búðingur	boo-theen-görr
chocolate	súkkulaði	sooh-kö-lah-thi
stewed fruit	ávaxtagrautur	ow-vahg-stah-grreör-törr

Drinks (non-alcoholic)

coffee (white/ black)	kaffi (með mjólk/ svart)	kahf-fi (mehth myolk/ svahrrt)
fruit juice	ávaxtasafi	ow-vahgs-tah-sah-vi
ice	klaki	klah-kyi
soft drinks	gosdrykkir	gos-drrih-kyirr
tea	te	teh
water	vatn	vahdn

> **Fast Talk** **Kaffi (Coffee)**
> Life without kaffi (coffee) is unthinkable in Iceland. Cafes and petrol stations will usually have an urn of filter coffee by the counter, and some shops offer complimentary cups of it to customers. Snug European-style cafes selling espresso, latte, cappuccino and mocha are ever-more popular, popping up even in the most isolated one-horse hamlets (the coffee isn't always good, though). Tea is available, but ranks a very poor second choice – the brand sitting on most supermarket shelves makes a feeble brew.

Alcoholic Drinks

aqua vitae (brandy; black death)	brennivín	brreh-ni-veen
beer	bjór	byohrr
cognac	koníak	ko-nee-ahk
liqueur	líkjör	lee-kyer
whisky	whisky	vis-kee
red/white wine	rauðvín/hvítvín	rreörth-veen/ kveet-veen

Menu Decoder

Starters

flatkökur og hangikjöt flahd-ker-körr og hown-gyi-kyert thin unsweet bread made of rye flour, eaten with butter and slices of smoked lamb
grafinn lax grrahv-inn lahks gravlax
harðfiskur harrth-fis-görr dried fish, stockfish

Main Meals

bjúgu byoo-ö smoked minced meat sausage. Served hot or cold with potatoes in white sauce.
flatkökur flaht-ker-körr rye pancakes, also popular with hangikjöt
hangikjöt hown-gyi-kyert smoked lamb, leg or shoulder. Served hot or cold, with potatoes, bechamel sauce and green peas. Also popular as luncheon meat.
harðfiskur hahrrth-fis-körr dried fish; haddock, cod or catfish. It does not require cooking but is enjoyed as snack food, often spread with a little butter.
kjötsúpa kyert-soo-pah soup, made of a small quantity of vegetables and a large quantity of lamb meat and rice. Always served hot.
saltkjöt sahlt-kyert salted lamb/mutton, served with potatoes or swede turnips and often accompanied by split pea soup
slátur slow-törr blood and liver puddings. Prepared in the months of September and October, when slaughtering is at its peak. Blood pudding, **blóðmör** (blohth-mehrr), and liver pudding, **lifrarpylsa** (liv-rrahrr-pil-sah), are eaten sliced hot or cold. Traditionally, the slátur that could not be eaten fresh was pickled in whey and enjoyed throughout the winter months.
svið svith singed sheep heads. Eaten hot or cold, with either plain boiled potatoes, mashed potatoes or swede turnips. The pressed and gelled variety is popular for packed lunches.
seytt rúgbrauð saiht rroo-brreörth cooked rye bread, moist and chewy. Popular with hangikjöt.

Desserts

pönnukökur með sykri eða með sultu og rjóma pern-nö-ker-körr mehth si-grri ehthah mehth súl-tö og rryo-mah pancakes with sugar or with jam and cream
skyr skyirr dairy product similar to yoghurt, it's very low in fat. Eaten as dessert with sugar and milk and with fresh berries, when in season.

Sightseeing & Entertainment

≡ Fast Phrases

What time does it open/close?	Klukkan hvað opnar/lokar? klök-ahn kvahth op-nahrr/lok-ahrr?
Is there a local entertainment guide?	Er til bæklingur umskemmtanir hér á staðnum? ehrr til baik-leen-görr öm skiehm-tah-nirr hyehrr ow stahth-nöm?
Can I take photographs?	Má ég taka myndir? mow yehkh tah-kah mind-irr?

Planning

Do you have a guidebook/local map?	Áttu ferðahandbók/ kort af staðnum? owt-ö fehrrth-ah-hahnd-bohk/ korrt ahv stahth-nöm?
What are the main attractions?	Hvað er markvert að sjá? kvahth ehrr mahrrk-vehrrt ahth syow?

44

Local Knowledge — Festivals

A very old tradition in Iceland is celebrating the first day of summer, sumardagurinn fyrsti. It's an old custom to give sumargjöf (a summer gift) to close relatives.

Sautjándi júní, 17 June, is Iceland's National Independence Day. It's celebrated in front of the Parliament where the fjallkona, a female symbol of Iceland (usually a young actress in national costume), recites a poem.

The most important day of preparation for Jólin (Christmas), is 23 December, called Þorláksmessa after the only officially canonised Icelandic saint. The main Christmas celebration starts with a Christmas church service on Christmas Eve, aðfangadagskvöld, followed by a family dinner. To wish someone a merry Christmas you say gleðileg jól. During Þorri, the fourth month of winter (from mid-January to mid-February), it's common to hold a party called þorrablót, where people gather to sing and eat traditional Icelandic food.

Seven weeks before Easter is bolludagur 'bun-day', so-called because people are supposed to have all kinds of buns on this day. Children wake their parents in the morning with bolluvöndur, a decorated birch-rod. The last day before the beginning of the traditional Lenten fast (Shrove Tuesday) is sprengidagur. The name refers to sprenging (explosion) because people are supposed to eat as much saltkjöt og baunir (salted lamb/mutton, served with split pea soup) as they can, even so much that they may 'explode'.

Questions

What is that?	Hvað er þetta? kvahth ehrr <u>theh</u>-dah?
How old is it?	Hvað er það gamalt? kvahth ehrr <u>thath</u> gahm-ahlt?

Can I take photographs?	Má ég taka myndir?
	mow yehkk tah-kah mind-irr?
What time does it open/close?	Klukkan hvað opnar/lokar?
	klök-ahn kvahth op-nahrr/lok-ahrr?

Going Out

What's there to do in the evenings?	Hvað er hægt að gera á kvöldin?
	kvahth ehrr haikht ahth gyeh-rra ow kverl-din?
Is there a local entertainment guide?	Er til bæklingur um skemmtanir hér á staðnum?
	ehrr til baik-leen-görr öm skyehm-tah-nirr hyehrr ow stahth-növm?

PHRASE BUILDER

I feel like going to a/the ...	Mig langar að fara ...	mig lowngarr ahth fahrrah ...
cinema	í bíó	ee bee-oh
opera	í óperuna	ee oh-peh-rrö-nah
theatre	í leikhús	ee layk-hoos
bar	á bar	ow bahrr
cafe	á kaffihús	ow kahffi-hoos
concert/gig	á tónleika	ow tohn-lay-kah
disco	á diskótek	ow diskoh-tehk
nightclub	á næturklúbb	ow nai-törr-kloobb
restaurant	á veitingastað	ow vay-teen-gah-stahth

Interests

What are your interests?	Hver eru áhugamálin þín?	kvehrr eh-rrö <u>th</u>een ow-högah-mowl?
What sports do you play?	Hvaða íþróttir stundar þú?	kvah-thah ee-<u>th</u>rroh-tirr stön-dahrr <u>th</u>oo?

INTERESTS

art	listir	lis-tirr
basketball	körfubolti	ker-fö-bol-ti
collecting things	að safna hlutum	ahth sab-nah hlö-töm
dancing	að dansa	ahth dahnsah
food	matur	mah-törr
football	fótbolti	fohd-bol-ti
hiking	gönguferðir	geörn-gö-fehrr-thirr
martial arts	bardaga-íþróttir	bahrr-dahgah-ee-throh-tirr
movies	kvikmyndir	kvik-min-dirr
music	tónlist	tohn-list
photography	ljósmyndun	lyohs-min-dön
reading	lestur	lehs-törr
shopping	að fara í búðir	ahth fah-rrah ee boo-thirr
skiing	að fara á skíði	ahth fah-rrah ow skee-thi
swimming	sund	sund
tennis	tehn-nis	tennis
travelling	að ferðast	ahth fehrr-thahst
TV	sjónvarp	syohn-vahrrp

Shopping

≡ Fast Phrases

I'd like to buy ...	Mig langar að kaupa ... mikh lown-khahrr ahth keör-pah ...
Can you write down the price?	Gætir þú skrifað niður verðið? gyeht-irr-ö skrri-vahth nith-örr vehrrthith?

Shops

general store, shop	búð booth
laundry	þvottahús thvo-hdah-hoos
market	markaður mahrr-kahth-örr
newsagency/stationers	blaðasala/bókabúð blah-thah-sah-lah/boh-kah-booth
pharmacy	apótek ahp-oh-tehk
shoe shop	skóbúð skoh-booth

Souvenirs

Reykjavík is Iceland's shopping hub, but creativity and first-rate craftsmanship is on display countrywide, Even in the smallest towns, galleries and stores (plus guesthouses, cafes and museums) exhibit and sell the output of talented locals. Knitwear – especially the lopapeysa, the signature woollen sweater – is ubiquitous, but photography, artwork, fashion and design objects may also catch your eye. Books, foodstuffs and local booze make fine souvenirs.

Before purchasing knitwear, do look to see where it was made. A number of stores stock lopapeysur 'made in China from Icelandic wool' or words to that effect.

supermarket	stórmarkaður	stohrr-mahrr-kahth-örr
vegetable shop	grænmetisbúð	grrain-meht-is-booth

Essential Groceries

batteries	rafhlöður	rrahv-hler-thör
bread	brauð	brreörth
butter	smjör	smyer-rr
cheese	ostur	os-törr
chocolate	súkkulaði	sooh-kö-lah-thi
eggs	egg	ehg
flour	hveiti	kvay-ti
gas cylinder	gashylki	gahs-hihl-kyi
honey	hunang	hö-nowng
marmalade	marmelaði	mahrr-meh-lah-thi

Fast Talk	**Bargaining**

Bargaining is not an accepted practice. You are expected to pay advertised rates.

matches	eldspýtur	ehld-spee-törr
milk	mjólk	myohlk
olive oil	ólífuolía	oh-lee-vö-o-lee-ah
pepper	pipar	pi-pahrr
salt	salt	sahlt
shampoo	sjampó	syahm-poh
soap	sápa	sow-pah
sugar	sykur	si-körr
toilet paper	klósettpappír	kloh-seht-pah-pirr
toothbrush	tannbursti	tahn-bös-di
washing powder	þottaduft	tvoh-tah-düft

Clothing

clothing	föt	fert
coat	kápa	kow-pah
dress	kjóll	kyohdl
jacket	jakki	yah-kyi
jumper/sweater	peysa	pay-sah
shirt	skyrta	skyirr-tah
shoes	skór	skohrr
skirt	pils	pils
trousers	buxur	bög-sörr

Materials

cotton	bómull	boh-mödl
handmade	handgert	hahnd-gyehrrt
leather	leður	leh-thörr
brass	messing	oorr mehs-eeng
gold	gull	güdl
silver	silfur	sil-vörr
flax	hör	herrr
silk	silki	sil-kyi
wool	ull	ödl

Colours

black	svart	svahrrt
blue	blátt	blowt
brown	brúnt	brroont
green	grænt	grraint

Local Knowledge **Shops**

What is the best place for shopping?	Hvar er best að versla?
	kvahrr ehr behst ath vehrr-sdla
Where would you go for souvenirs?	Hvar get ég keypt minjagripi?
	kvahrr gyeht yekh kyayft min-yah-grri-bi

red	rautt	rreört
white	hvítt	kveet
yellow	gult	gölt

Toiletries

comb	greiða	grray-thah
condoms	smokkar	smok-ahrr
deodorant	svitalyktareyðir	svi-tah-likt-ahrr-ay-thirr
razor	rakvél	rrahk-vyehl
sanitary napkins	dömubindi	der-mö-bin-di
shampoo	sjampó	syahm-poh
shaving cream	raksápa	rrahk-sow-pah
soap	sápa	sow-pah
tampons	túrtappar	toorr-tahp-ahr

Local Knowledge

Tax-free Shopping

Anyone who has a permanent address outside Iceland can claim a tax refund on purchases when they spend more than kr6000 at a single point of sale. Look for stores with a 'tax-free shopping' sign in the window, and ask for a form at the register.

Before you check in for your departing flight at Keflavík, go to the refund office at Arion Banki and present your completed tax-free form, passport, receipts/invoices and purchases. Make sure the goods are unused. Opening hours of the office match flight schedules.

If you're departing Iceland from Reykjavík airport or a harbour, go to the customs office before check-in.

Full details outlined at www.globalblue.com.

tissues	bréfþurrkur	brryehv-<u>th</u>örr-körr
toilet paper	klósettpappír	kloh-seht-pah-peer
toothpaste	tannkrem	tahn-krrehm

Stationery & Publications

map	kort	korrt
newspaper (in English)	dagblað (á ensku)	dakh-blahth (ow ehn-skö)
paper	pappír	pah-peer
pen (ballpoint)	penni/kúlupenni	pehn-ni/koo-lö-pehn-ni

Sizes & Comparisons

big	stórt	stohrrt
small	lítið	lee-tith
heavy	þungt	<u>th</u>oont
light	létt	lyeht
less	minna	mi-nah
more	meira	may-rrah

Practicalities

Fast Phrases

Could you help me please?	Gætir þú hjálpað mér? gyai-tirr <u>thoo</u> hyowlp-ahth myehrr?
What time does it open/ close?	Hvenær er opnað/ lokað? kveh-nairr ehrr op-nahth/ lo-kahth?
Where are the toilets?	Hvar er snyrtingin?/ Hvar er klósettið? kvahrr ehrr snirrt-inkh-in?/ kvahrr ehrr kloh-seht-ith?

Banking

I want to exchange some money/ travellers cheques.	Ég þarf að skipta peningum/ferðatékkum. yehkh <u>thahrrf</u> ahth skif-dah pehn-inkh-öm/fehrrth-ah-tyehköm
What is the exchange rate?	Hvert er gengið? kvehrrt ehrr gehngith?
How many kronas per dollar?	Hvað eru margar krónur í dollaranum? kvahth ehrr-ö mahrr-gahrr krrohn-örr ee dol-ah-rrah-nöm?

USEFUL WORDS

bank notes	seðlar	sehth-lahrr
cashier	gjaldkeri	gyahld-kehrr-i
coins	smámynt; klink	smow-mint; kleenkh
credit card	greiðslukort	grrayth-slö-korrt
exchange	skipta	skif-dah
loose change	reiðufé	rrayth-ö-fyeh
signature	undirskrift	ön-dirr-skrrift

Telephone

I want to ring ...	Ég þarf að hringja ... yehkh <u>th</u>ahrrv ahth hrreen-gya ...
The number is ...	Númerið er ... noo-mehrr-ith ehrr ...
How much does a three-minute call cost?	Hvað kostar þriggja mínútna samtal? kvahth kos-dahrr <u>th</u>rri-khjah-meen-oot-nah sahm-tahl?
How much does each extra minute cost?	Hvað kostar hver mínúta? kvahth kos-dahrr kvehrr meen-oo-tah?
I'd like to speak to (Jón Pálsson).	Gæti ég fengið að tala við (Jón Pálsson)? gyai-ti yehkh fayn-gith ahth tahlah vith (yohn powls-sohn)?
I want to make a reverse-charges phone call.	Ég ætla að hringja og viðtakandi borgar. yehkh ait-lah ahth hrreen-khyah okh vith-tahk-ahn-di borr-gahrr
It's engaged.	Það er á tali. <u>th</u>ahth ehrr ow tah-li
I've been cut off.	Það slitnaði. <u>th</u>ahth slit-nahth-i

55

PHRASE BUILDER

I'm looking for a/the ...	Ég er að leita að ...	yehkh ehrr ahth lay-tah ahth ...
bank	banka	bown-kah
city centre	miðbænum	mith-bai-nöm
... embassy	... sendiráðinu	... sehn-di-rrow-thi-nö
hotel	hótelinu mínu	hoh-tehl-i-nö mee-nö
market	markaðnum	mahrrk-ahth-nöm
police	lögreglunni	lerkh-rrehgl-ö-ni
post office	pósthúsinu	pohst-hoos-i-nö
public toilet	almennings-salerni	ahl-mehn-inkhs-sahl-ehrr-dni
tourist information office	upplýsinga-þjónustu fyrir ferðafólk	öp-lees-een-gah-thjohn-öst-ö firr-irr fehrrth-ah-fohlk

Internet

Where can I get Internet access?	Hvar gæti ég fengið að nota internetið? kvahr gyai-di yehkh fayn-gyith ahth noh-tah in-tehrr-neh-tith?
I'd like to send an email.	Mig langar að senda tölvupóst. Mig lown-guhrr ahth sen-duh terl-vü-pohst
Is there wifi access here?	Eruð þið með wifi? ehrr-öth thith mehth vai-fai
What's the wifi password?	Hvað er lykilorðið fyrir netið? kvahth ehrr li-kyil-orrth-ith firr-irr neht-ith

Local Knowledge

Television

Iceland had just one TV channel until 1988 – and even that went off air on Thursdays so that citizens could do something more productive instead. It also went on summer vacation! It's said that most children born before 1988 were conceived on a Thursday...

Post

I'd like some stamps.	Ég ætla að fá nokkur frímerki. yehkh aid-lah ahth fow nok örr frree-mehrr-gi
How much does it cost to send this to ...?	Hvað kostar að senda þetta til ...? kvahth kos-dahrr ahth sehn-dah theh-dah til ...?
airmail	flugpóstur flookh-pohst-örr
envelope	umslag öm-slahkh
mailbox	póstkassi pohst-kahss-i

PHRASE BUILDER

I'd like to send a ...	Ég ætla að senda ...	yehkh ait-lah ahth sehn-dah ...
letter	bréf	brryehv
postcard	kort	korrt
parcel	pakka	pahk-ah
telegram	skeyti	skay-ti

registered mail	ábyrgðarpóstur
	ow-birrth-ahrr-pohst-örr
surface mail/sea mail	sjópóstur
	syoh-pohst-örr

Emergencies

Help!	Hjálp!
	hyowlp!
Go away!	Farðu!
	fahrr-thö!
Thief!	þjófur!
	thyoh-vörr!
There's been an accident!	Það hefur orðið slys!
	thahth hehf-örr orrth-ith slis!
Call a doctor/an ambulance!	Náið í lækni/sjúkrabíl!
	now-ith ee laik-nisyook-rrah beel!
I've been raped.	Mér var nauðgað.
	myehrr vahrr neörth-gahth
I've been robbed!	Ég var rænd/-ur! (f/m)
	yehkh vahrr rraind/rrain-dörr!
Call the police!	Náið í lögregluna!
	nowith ee lerg-rrehgl-ön-ah!
Where is the police station?	Hvar er lögreglustöðin?
	kvahrr ehrr lerkh-rrehkh-lö-sterth-in?
I'm/My friend is ill.	Ég er/vinur minn er veikur.
	yehkh ehrr/vin-örr min ehrr vay-körr
I'm lost.	Ég er villt/-ur. (f/m)
	yehkh ehrr vilt/vilt-örr
Where are the toilets?	Hvar er snyrtingin?/Hvar er klósettið?
	kvahrr ehrr snirrt-inkh-in?/kvahrr ehrr kloh-seht-ith?

58

Could you help me please?	Gætir þú hjálpað mér?
	gyai-tirr <u>thoo</u> hyowlp-ahth myehrr?
Could I please use the telephone?	Gæti ég fengið að hringja?
	gyai-ti yehkh fayn-khith ahth hrrin-gyah?
I'm sorry.	Mér þykir það leitt.
	myehrr <u>thik</u>-irr <u>th</u>ahth layht
I didn't realise I was doing anything wrong.	Ég vissi ekki að ég væri að leitthvað aytkvahth gera rangt.
	yehkh vi-si ehk-i ahth yehkh vai-rri ahth gyeh-rrah rrow-nt
I didn't do it.	Ég gerði það ekki.
	yehkh gyehrr-thi <u>th</u>ahth ehk-i
I wish to contact my embassy/consulate.	Ég vil hafa samband við sendiráð mitt/ræðismann minn.
	yehkh vil hah-vah sahm-bahnd vith sehndi-rrowth mit/ rraith-is-mahn min
I speak English.	Ég tala ensku.
	yehkh tah-lah ehn-skö

PHRASE BUILDER

My... was stolen.	... var stolið.	... vahrr sto-lith
I've lost my ...	Ég týndi ...	yehkh teen-di ...
bags	töskunum mínum	ter-skö-nöm mee-nöm
handbag	handtöskunni minni	hahnd-tersk-ön-i mi-ni
money	peningunum mínum	pehn-eeng-ön-öm mee-nöm
travellers cheques	ferðatékkunum mínum	fehrrth-ah-tyeh-kö-nöm mee-nöm
passport	vegabréfinu mínu	vehg-ah-brryeh-vi-nö mee-nö

59

| I have medical insurance. | Ég er með sjúkratryggingu.
yehkh ehrr mehth syook-rrah-trrikh-een-gö |
| My possessions are insured. | Eigur mínar eru tryggðar.
aykh-örr meen-ahrr ehrr-ö trrikhth-arr |

Paperwork

address	heimilisfang hay-mil-is-fowng
age	aldur ahld-örr
birth certificate	fæðingarvottorð faith-ing-ahrr-vot-orrth
car owner's title	eignarvottorð ayg-nahrr-vot-orrth
car registration	bifreiðaskoðun biv-rrayth-ah-skoth-ön
customs	tollskoðun todl-skoth-ön
date of birth	fæðingardagur faith-ing-ahrr-dahkh-örr
driver's licence	ökuskírteini er-kö-skeer-tay-ni
identification	skilríki skil-rree-ki
immigration	vegabréfsskoðun vehkh-ah- brryehvs-skoth-ön
name	nafn nahbn
nationality	þjóðerni thyohth-ehrr-dni

Local Knowledge

What's in a Name?

There's an official list of names that Icelanders are permitted to call their children, and any additions to this list have to be approved by the Icelandic Naming Committee. Among the requirements for approval are that given names must be 'capable of having Icelandic grammatical endings', and shall not 'conflict with the linguistic structure of Iceland'.

passport (number)	vegabréf (snúmer) vehkh-ah-brryehv (s-noo-ehrr)
place of birth	fæðingarstaður faith-ing-ahrr-stahth-örr
profession	atvinna aht-vin-ah
reason for travel	ástæða ferðalagsins ow-staith-ah fehrrth-ah-lahkhs-ins
religion	trú trroo
sex	kyn kin
tourist card	ferðamannaspjald fehrrth-ah- mahn-ah-spyahld
visa	vegabréfsáritun vehkh-ah- brryehvs-ow-rrit-ön

PHRASE BUILDER

Where is a ...?	Hvar er ...?	kvahrr ehrr ...?
doctor	læknir	laik-nirr
hospital	sjúkrahús	syook-rrah-hoos
chemist	apótek	ah-poh-tehk
dentist	tannlæknir	tahn-laik-nirr

Local Knowledge

Healthcare

The standard of healthcare in Iceland is extremely high, and English is widely spoken by doctors and medical-clinic staff. Note, however, that there are limited services outside larger urban areas.

For minor ailments, pharmacists can dispense valuable advice and over-the-counter medication; pharmacies can be identified by the sign apótek. Pharmacists can also advise as to when more specialised help is required.

Medical care can be obtained by visiting a healthcare centre, called heilsugæslustöð. Find details of centres in greater Reykjavík at www.heilsugaeslan.is; in regional areas, ask at a tourist office or your accommodation for advice on the closest healthcare centre.

For more detailed information on healthcare for visitors, see www.sjukra.is/english/tourists.

Health

Could I see a female doctor?	Gæti ég fengið að tala við kvenlækni?
	gyai-ti yehkh fayn-gith ahth tah-lah vith kvehn lai-ni?
What's the matter?	Hvað er að?
	kvahth ehrr ahth?

PHRASE BUILDER

I'm ...	Ég er ...	yehkh ehrr ...
asthmatic	með asma	mehth ahs-mah
diabetic	sykursjúkur	sik-örr-syoo-körr
epileptic	flogaveikur	flokh-ah-vay-körr
sunburnt	sólbrunninn	sohl-brrön-in

I have (a)...	Ég er með ...	yehkh ehrr mehth ...
cold	kvef	kvehf
constipation	harðlífi	hahrrth-lee-vi
diarrhoea	niðurgang	nith-örr-gowng
fever	hita	hi-tah
headache	höfuðverk	her-vöth-vehrrk
indigestion	meltingar-truflun	mehlt-eeng-ahrr-trröb-lön
influenza	flensu	flehn-sö
low/high blood pressure	lágan/háan blóðþrýsting	low-ahn/how-ahn blohth-thrreest-eeng
sore throat	hálsbólgu	howls-bohl-gö
sprain	tognun	tokh-nön
stomachache	magaverk	mahkh-ah-vehrrk
sunburn	sólbruni	sohl-brrö-ni

Where does it hurt?	Hvar finnur þú til? kvahrr fin-örr thoo til?
It hurts here.	Mig verkjar hér. mikh vehrrk-yahrr hyehrr

Parts of the Body

ankle	ökkli erh-kli
arm	handleggur hahnd-lehgg-örr
back	bak bahk

chest	bringa brreeng-ah
ear	eyra ay-rrah
eye	auga eör-gah
finger	fingur feen-görr
feet/legs	fætur fai-törr
hands	hendur hehn-dörr
head	höfuð her-vöth
heart	hjarta hyarr-tah
hips	mjaðmir myath-mirr
mouth	munnur mön-nörr
neck	háls howls
ribs	rifbein rriv-bayn
skin	húð hooth
stomach	magi mai-i
teeth	tennur tehn-nörr
thighs	læri lai-rri

Useful Phrases

I'm allergic to antibiotics/ penicillin.	Ég er með ofnæmi fyrir fúkalyfjum/ pensilíni.
	yehkh ehrr mehth ov-nai-mi firr-irr foo-kah-liv-yöm/ pehn-si-lee-ni
I'm pregnant.	Ég er ófrísk.
	yehkh ehrr oh-frreesk
I've been vaccinated.	Ég fékk ónæmissprautu.
	yehkh fyehk oh-nai-mis-sprreör-tö
I feel better/worse.	Mér líður betur/verr.
	myehrr leeth-örr beh-törr/vehrr

At the Chemist

| I need medication for ... | Ég þarf lyf við ... |
| | yehkh <u>tha</u>hrrf lif vith ... |

USEFUL WORDS
....

antibiotics	fúkalyf	foo-kah-lif
antiseptic	sótthreinsandi	soht-hrrayns-ahndi
blood pressure	blóðþrýstingur	blohth-<u>th</u>rreest-ing-örr
blood test	blóðprufa	blohth-prrövah
contraceptive	getnaðarvörn	gyeht-nahth-ahrr-verdn
injection	sprauta	sprreör-tah
medicine	lyf	lif
menstruation	blæðingar	blaith-eeng-ahrr
nausea	ógleði	oh-khleh-thi
toothache	tannpína	tahn-pee-nah

| I have a prescription. | Ég er með lyfseðil.
yehkh ehrr mehth lif-sehth-il |

At the Dentist

I have a toothache.	Ég er með tannpínu. yehkh ehrr mehth tahn-pee-nö
I've lost a filling.	Ég missti fyllingu. yehkh mis-ti fid-leen-gö
I've broken a tooth.	Ég braut tönn. yehkh brreört tern
My gums hurt.	Mig verkjar í tann-holdið. mikh vehrr-kyarr ee tahn-hol-dith
Please give me an anaesthetic.	Gerðu svo velað deyfa mig. gyehrr-thö svo vehl ath day-vah mikh

Abbreviations

f.h./e.h. – fyrir hádegi/eftir hádegi	am/pm
h.f. – hlutafélag	Ltd./Inc.
Strætó bs	Reykjavík Municipal Bus Company
f.kr./e.kr.	BC/AD
frk. – fröken	Miss
frú	Mrs
hr. – herra	Mr/Sir
Rvk.	Reykjavík
FÍB – Félag íslensk-ra bifreiðaeigenda	The Icelandic Automobile Association
kl. – klukkan	o'clock

km/klst. – kílóme-trar á klukkustund	kilometres per hour
kr. – króna	crown (Icelandic monetary unit)
v. – við	at
vsk. – virðisau-kaskattur	tax (included in the price on all goods and services)
t.h. – til hægri	to the right (used in addresses)
t.v. – til vinstri	to the left (used in addresses)
vs. – vinnusími	telephone at work
hs. – heimasími	telephone at home
(1.) h. – hæð	(1st) floor

Dictionary

ENGLISH *to* ICELANDIC

a

accommodation gisting gist-eeng
account reikning rrayk-neen-görr
aeroplane flugvél flükh-vyehl
afternoon síðdegi seeth-day-yi
air-conditioned loftræsing lofd-rais-eeng
airport flugvöllur flükh-verdlörr
airport tax flugvallaskattur flükh-vahdl-ah-skaht-örr
alarm clock vekjaraklukka veh-gyah-rrah-klük-ah
alcohol áfengi ow-fayng-yi
antique antík ahn-teek
appointment stefnumót sdehb-nü-moht
arrivals komur ko-mör
art gallery listagallerí list-ah-gahll-ehrr-ee
ashtray öskubakki ersk-ü-bahk-i
at hjá hyow
ATM hraðbanki hrrahth-bown-gyi
autumn haust heörst

b

baby smábarn smow-bahdn
back (body) bak bahg
backpack bakpoki bahg-pok-yi
bad vont vont
bag poki pok-yi
baggage farangur far-owng-örr
baggage allowance farangursheimild far-owng-örrs-hay-mild
baggage claim farangursband far-owng-örrs-bahnd
bakery bakarí bah-ka-rree
Band-Aid plástur plowst-örr
bank banki bownk-yi
bank account bankabók bownk-ah-bohk
bath bað bahth
bathroom baðherbergi bahth-hehrr-behrr-gyi
battery rafhlaða rahv-hlahth-ah
beach strönd strernd
beautiful falleg/ur (f/m) fahdl-ekh/-ör
beauty salon snyrtistofa snirr-di-stov-ah

68

bed rúm rroom
bed linen rúmföt rroom-fert
bedroom svefnherbergi svehbn-hehrr-behrr-gyi
beer bjór byohrr
bicycle reiðhjól rrayth-hyohl
big stór stohrr
bill reikningur rrayk-neeng-örr
birthday afmæli ahv-mai-li
black svört/svartur (f/m) svehrrt/svahrrt-örr
blanket teppi teh-bi
blood group blóðflokkur blohth-flog-örr
blue blá/r (f/m) blow/rr
boarding house heimagisting haym-ah-gist-eeng
boarding pass farmiði fahrr-mith-i
boat bátur bow-törr
book bók bohk
book (make a booking) bóka bohk-ah
booked up fullbókað fúdl-bohk-ahth
bookshop bókabúð bohk-ah-booth
border landamæri lahn-da-mai-rri
bottle flaska flahs-kah
box box box
boy strákur strrow-körr
boyfriend kærasti kyairr-ahst-i
bra brjóstahaldari brryohst-ah-hahldahrr-i
brakes bremsur brrehms-ör
bread brauð breörth
briefcase skjalataska skyah-lah-tahsk-ah
broken bilað/ur (f/m) bil-ahth/-örr
brother bróðir brrohht-irr
brown brún/n (f/m) brroon/brroodn
building bygging big-eeng
bus (city) strætó strrai-toh
bus (intercity) rúta rroo-tah
bus station umferðarmiðstöð ümferrth-ahrr-mith-sterth
bus stop stoppistöð stop-i-sterr-th
business viðskipti vith-skift-i
business class viðskiptafarrými vith-skift-ah-fahrr-rree-mi

busy upptekin/n (f/m) üp-tehk-yin
butcher's shop kjötbúð kyerrt-booth

C

cafe kaffihús kahff-i-hoos
call hringja hrreeng-yah
camera myndavél mind-ah-vyehl
can (tin) dós dohs
cancel hætta við hait-ah vith
car bíll beedl
car hire bílaleiga bee-lah-laykh-ah
car registration skráningarskírteini skrrow-neeng-ahrr-skeerr-tay-ni
cash reiðufé rray-thö-fyeh
cashier gjaldkeri gyahld-kyehrr-i
chairlift (skiing) skíðalyfta skee-tha-lift-ah
change til baka til bah-kah
change (coins) skiptimynt skif-ti-mint
change (money) peningar til baka peh-neeng-ahrr til bah-kah
check kvittun kvit-ön
check (banking) kvittun kvit-ön
check-in (desk) innritun in-rrit-ön
cheque ávísun ow-vees-ön
child barn bahdn
church kirkja kirr-gyah
cigarette lighter kveikjari kvay-gyahrr-i
city borg borrg
city centre miðborg mith-borrg
clean hrein/n (f/m) hrrayn/hrraydn
cleaning hreinsun hrrayns-ön
cloakroom fatageymsla faht-ah-gaym-sdlah
closed lokað lok-ahth
clothing föt fert
coat kápa kow-pah
coffee kaffi kahf-i
coins klink kleenk
cold kalt kahlt
comfortable þægilegt thai-yi-lekht
company fyrirtæki fi-rrirr-tai-kyi
computer tölva terl-vah
condom smokkur smok-örr

confirm (a booking) staðfesta (bókun) stahth-fehst-ah (bohk-ön)
connection samband sahm-bahnd
convenience store kjörbúð kyerr-booth
cook elda ehl-dah
cool kúl kool
cough hósti hohst-i
countryside sveitin svay-tin
cover charge aðgangseyrir ath-gowngs-ayrr-irr
crafts handverk hahnd-verrk
credit card kreditkort krre-dit-korrt
currency exchange gjaldmiðlaskipti gyahld-mith-lah-skif-ti
customs tollur todl-örr

d

daily daglega dahkh-lehkh-ah
date dagsetning dahkh-seht-neeng
date of birth fæðingardagur faith-eeng-ahrr-dahkh-örr
daughter dóttir doht-irr
day dagur dahkh-örr
day before yesterday í fyrradag ee firr-ah-dahkh
delay seinkun saynk-ön
delicatessen sælkeraverslun sail-kyeh-rrah-ves-dlön
depart fara fah-rrah
department store stórverslun stohrr-ves-dlön
departure brottför brrot-ferrr
deposit trygging trrig-eeng
diaper bleyja blay-yah
dictionary orðabók orrth-ah-bohk
dining car veitingavagn vay-teeng-ah-vahgn
dinner kvöldmatur kverld-maht-örr
direct beint baynt
dirty skítugt skee-tökht
discount afsláttur av-slowt-örr
dish diskur disk-örr
doctor læknir laik-nirr
dog hundur hünd-örr

double bed tvíbreitt rúm tvee-brrayt rroom
double room tvöfalt herbergi tver-fahlt hehrr-behrr-gyi
dress kjóll kyohdl
drink drekka drrehk-ah
drink (beverage) drykkur drrik-örr
drivers licence ökuskírteini erk-ö-skeerr-tayn-i
drunk full/ur (f/m) füdl/-örr
dry þurrt thürrt

e

each hver kvehrr
early snemma sdnehmm-ah
east austur eörst-örr
eat borða borrth-ah
economy class almennt farrými ahl-mehnt fahrr-rreemi
elevator lyfta lif-tah
embassy sendiráð sehn-di-rrowth
English enska ehn-skah
enough nóg noh
entry inngangur in-gowng-örr
envelope umslag üm-sdlag
evening kvöld kverld
every sérhvert syehrr-kvehrrt
everything allt ahlt
excess (baggage) umfram (farangur) üm-frrahm (fahrr-owng-ör)
exchange skipta skif-tah
exhibition sýning see-neeng
exit útgangur oot-gowng-ör
expensive dýrt deerrt
express (mail) hrað (póstur) hrrath (pohst-ör)

f

fall detta deht-ah
family fjölskylda fjerl-skild-ah
fare fargjald fahrr-gyahld
fashion tíska teesk-ah
fast hratt hrraht
father pabbi pahb-i

ferry ferja fehrr-yah
fever hiti hi-ti
film (for camera) filma (fyrir myndavél) fil-mah (firr-irr mind-ah-vyehl)
fine (penalty) sekt (hegning) sehkht
finger putti püt-i
first class fyrsta farrými firrst-ah fahrr-rreem-i
fish shop fiskbúð fisk-booth
flea market flóamarkaður floh-ah-mahrrk-ahth-örr
flight flug flükh
floor (storey) hæð haith
flu flensa flehn-sah
footpath göngustígur geörng-ö-steekh-örr
foreign útlensk/ur (f/m) ootlehnsk/-örr
forest skógur skohkh-örr
free (at liberty) frjálst (óhindrað) frryowlst (oh-hind-rraht)
free (gratis) ókeypis (gefins) oh-kay-pis (gyeh-vins)
fresh ferskt fehrrst
friend vinur vin-örr

g

garden garður gahrrth-örr
gas gas gahs
gift gjöf gyerv
girl stelpa stehl-pah
girlfriend kærasta kairr-ahst-ah
glasses (spectacles) gleraugu glehrr-eörkh-ö
gloves hanskar hahn-skahr
go fara fah-rrah
go out fara út fah-rrah
go shopping fara að versla fah-rrah ath ves-dla
gold gull güdl
grateful þakklát/ur (f/m) thahk-low-törr
gray grá/r (f/m) grrow/-rr
green græn/n (f/m) grrain/grraidn
grocery verslun ves-dlön
guesthouse gistiheimili gist-i-hay-mi-li
guided tour leiðsögn layth-sergn

h

half helmingur helm-eeng-örr
handsome myndarleg/ur (f/m) mind-ahrr-lekh/örr
heated upphitað üp-hit-ahth
help hjálp hyowlp
here hérna hyehd-nah
highway þjóðvegur thyohth-vehkh-örr
hire leigja lay-yah
honeymoon brúðkaupsferðalag brrooth-keörps-ferrth-ah-lahkh
hospital sjúkrahús syook-rrah-hoos
hot heitt hayt
hotel hótel hoh-tehl
hour klukkustund klük-ö-stünd
husband eiginmaður ay-yin-mahth-örr

i

identification auðkenni eörth-kyehn-i
identification card (ID) skilríki skil-rreekyi
ill veik/ur (f/m) vayk/-örr
included innifalið in-i-fah-lith
information upplýsingar üp-lees-eeng-ahrr
insurance tryggingar trrig-eeng-ahrr
intermission hlé hlyeh
Internet cafe netkaffi neht-kahf-i
interpreter túlkur toolk-ör
itinerary ferðaáætlun ferrth-ah-ow-aitl-ön

j

jacket jakki yah-ekki
jeans gallabuxur gahl-ah-büx-ör
jewellery skartgripir skahrrt-grri-pirr
journey reisa rray-sah
jumper hettupeysa heh-tö-pay-sah

k

key lykill li-kyidl

kind blíð/ur (f/m) bleeth/-örr
kitchen eldhús ehld-hoos

l

lane akrein ahk-rrayn
large stórt stohrrt
last (previous) síðasta seeth-ahst-ah
late seint saynt
later seinna saydn-ah
launderette almenningsþvottahús ahl-mehn-eengs-thvot-ah-hoos
laundry (clothes) þvottur thvot-örr
leather leður lehth-örr
leave fara fah-rrah
left luggage (office) farangursgey-msla fahrr-own-görrs-gaym-sdlah
letter bréf brryehv
lift lyfta lif-tah
linen (material) lín (efni) leen (ehbni)
locked læst laist
look for leita að layt-ath
lost týnd/ur (f/m) teend/-örr
lost property office óskilamunir oh-skil-ah-mü-nirr
luggage farangur fahrr-own-görr
luggage lockers farangursskápar fahrr-own-görrs-skow-pahrr
lunch hádegismatur how-day-is-mah-tör

m

mail (postal system) póstur pohst-ör
make-up farði fahrr-thi
man karlmaður kahdl-mah-thörr
manager (restaurant, hotel) yfir-maður i-virr-mah-thörr
map (of country) (landa)kort (lahn-dah)korrt
map (of town) (bæjar)kort (baiy-ahrr)korrt
market markaður marrk-ath-ör
meal máltíð mowl-teeth
meat kjöt kyert
medicine (medication) lyf liv

metro station lestarstöð lehst-ahrr-sterth
midday miðdegi mith-day-i
midnight miðnætti mith-nait-i
milk mjólk myohlk
mobile phone farsími fahrr-see-mi
modem mótald moh-tahld
money peningar peh-neeng-ahrr
month mánuður mow-nüth-ör
morning morgun morr-gön
mother mamma mahm-ah
motorcycle mótorhjól moh-torr-hyohl
motorway hraðbraut hrrath-brreört
mountain fjall fyahdl
museum safn sahbn
music shop tónlistarbúð tohn-list-ahrr-booth

n

name nafn nahbn
napkin servíetta sehrr-vee-yeht-ah
nappy bleyja blay-yah
newsagent blaðasali blahth-ah-sah-li
newspaper fréttablað frryeht-ah-blath
next (month) næsti (mánuður) nais-ti (mow-nüth-örr)
nice indælt in-dailt
night nótt noht
night out út á lífið oot ow lee-vith
nightclub næturklúbbur nait-örr-kloob-örr
no vacancy ekkert laust eh-kyerrt leörst
non-smoking reyklaust rrayk-leörst
noon hádegi how-day-i
north norður norrth-ör
now núna noo-nah
number númer noo-mehrr

o

office skrifstofa skrivv-sto-vah
oil olía o-lee-ah

72

one-way ticket miði aðra leið mi-thi ahth-rrah layth
open opið op-ith
opening hours opnunartími op-nö-nahrr-tee-mi
orange (colour) appelsínugul/ur (f/m) ap-ehl-see-nö-gü-lörr
out of order bilað bi-lahth

p

painter málari mowl-ahrr-i
painting (a work) málverk mowl-vehrrk
painting (the art) málaralist mowl-ahrr-ah-list
pants buxur büx-örr
pantyhose sokkabuxur sok-ah-büx-örr
paper pappír pahp-eerr
party partí pahrr-tee
passenger farþegi fahrr-thay-i
passport vegabréf vehkh-ah-brryehf
passport number vegabréfsnúmer vehkh-ah-brryehfs-noom-ehrr
path leið layth
penknife vasahnífur vah-sah-hnee-vörr
pensioner ellilífeyrisþegi ehdl-i-leev-ayrr-is-thay-i
performance frammistaða frrahm-i-stahth-a
petrol bensín ben-seen
petrol station bensínstöð ben-seen-sterth
phone book símaskrá seem-ah-skrrow
phone box símaklefi seem-ah-kleh-vi
phone card símkort seem-korrt
phrasebook orðtakabók orth-tahk-ah-bowk
picnic lautarferð leört-ahrr-fehrth
pillow koddi kod-i
pillowcase koddaver kod-ah-vehrr
pink bleik/ur (f/m) blayk/-örr
platform pallur pahdl-örr

play (theatre) leikrit (leikhús) layk-rrit
police officer lögregluþjónn lerkh-rrehg-lö-thyohdn
police station lögreglustöð lerkh-rrehg-lö-sterth
post code póstnúmer pohst-noo-mehrr
post office pósthús pohst-hoos
postcard póstkort pohst-korrt
pound (money, weight) pund pünd
prescription lyfseðill liv-sehth-idl
present viðstödd/staddur (f/m) vith-sterd
price verð vehrrth

q

quick fljót/ur (f/m) flyoht/-örr

r

receipt kvittun kvit-ön
red rauð/ur (f/m) rreörth/-örr
refund endurgreiðsla ehn-dörr-grrayth-sdla
rent leiga lay-kha
repair viðgerð vith-gyehrth
retired á eftirlaunum ow ehf-tirr-leörr-nöm
return koma aftur ko-mah af-törr
return (ticket) miði báðar leiðir mi-thi bow-tharr lay-thirr
road vegur vehkh-ör
robbery rán rrown
room herbergi hehrr-behrr-gi
room number herbergisnúmer hehrr-behrr-gis-noom-ehrr
route vegur vehkh-ör

s

safe öruggt er-ökht
sea sjór syoh-rr
season árstíð owrrs-teeth
seat (place) sæti sai-ti

seatbelt sætisbelti sai-tis-behl-ti
self service sjálfsafgreiðsla sjowls-ahv-grayth-sdla
service þjónusta thyoh-nús-tah
service charge þjónustugjöld thyoh-nús-tu-gyerld
share deila day-lah
shirt skyrta skirrtah
shoe skór skohrr
shop búð booth
shopping centre verslunarmiðstöð ves-dlön-ahrr-mith-sterth
short (height) lág/ur lág/ur low/lowrr
show sýning see-neeng
shower sturta stürr-tah
sick veik/ur (f/m) vayk/-örr
silk silki sil-kyi
silver silfur sil-vörr
single (person) einhleyp/ur (f/m) ayn-hlayp/-örr
single room einstaklingsherbergi ayn-stahk-leengs-herr-berr-gyi
sister systir sis-tirr
size (general) stærð stairrth
skirt pils pils
sleeping bag svefnpoki svehbn-po-gyi
sleeping car svefnvagn svehbn-vahgn
slide (film) skyggna skig-nah
smoke reykur ray-körr
snack snarl snahrrdl
snow snjór snyohrr
socks sokkar sok-ahrr
son sonur son-örr
soon brátt browt
south suður sü-thörr
spring (season) vor vorr
square (town) torg torrg
stairway stigi stee-yi
stamp frímerki frree-mehrr-kyi
stationer's (shop) ritfangaverslun rrit-fown-gah-ves-dlön
stolen stolið sto-lith
stranger ókunnur maður oh-künn-örr mah-thörr
street gata gah-tah
student nemi neh-mi
subtitles texti tehx-ti

suitcase ferðataska fehrr-thah-tahs-kah
summer sumar sü-mahrr
supermarket stórmarkaður stohrr-mahrk-ahth-örr
surface mail (land) landpóstur lahn-pohst-örr
surface mail (sea) sjópóstur sjoh-pohst-örr
surname eftirnafn ef-dirr-nabn
sweater peysa pay-sah
swim synda sind-ah
swimming pool sundlaug sund-leörkh

t

tall há/r (f/m) how/rr
taxi stand leigubílastopp lay-khö-bee-lah-stop
teller gjaldkeri gyahld-kyeh-rri
ticket miði mi-thi
ticket machine miðavél mi-thah-vyehl
ticket office miðasala mi-thah-sah-lah
time tími tee-mi
timetable tímaáætlun tee-mah-ow-ait-lön
tip (gratuity) þjórfé thyohrr-fyeh
to til til
today í dag ee dahkh
together saman sah-mahn
tomorrow á morgun ow morr-gön
tour ferð fehrrth
tourist office upplýsingamiðstöð üp-lees-eeng-ah-mith-sterth
towel handklæði hand-klaith-i
town bær bairr
train station lestarstöð lehst-ahrr-sterth
transit lounge setustofa seht-u-stov-ah
travel agency ferðaskrifstofa fehrrth-ah-skriv-stov-ah
travellers cheque ferðatékki fehrrth-ah-tyehk-yi

trip ferð fehrrth
trousers buxur büx-örr
twin beds tvö rúm tver rroom

u

underwear nærföt nairr-fert

v

vacancy laust leörst
vacant laust leörst
vacation frí frree
validate staðfesta stahth-fehst-ah
vegetable grænmeti grrain-meht-i
view útsýni oot-seen-i

w

waiting room biðsalur bith-sahl-ör
walk ganga gowng-ah
warm hlý/r (f/m) hlee/rr
wash (something) þrífa three-vah
washing machine þvottavél thvot-ah-vyehl
watch horfa horr-va

water vatn vahthn
way leið layth
week vika vi-kah
west vestur vest-örr
what hvað kvath
when hvenær kvehnairr
where hvar kvahrr
which hver kvehrr
white hvít/ur (f/m) kveet/ör
who hver kvehrr
why af hverju ahf-kvehrr-yö
wife eiginkona ay-in-ko-nah
wifi wifi vai-fai
window gluggi glüg-yi
wine vín veen
winter vetur veh-törr
without án own
woman kona konah
wool ull üdl
wrong (direction) röng (leið) rreörng (layth)

y

year ár owrr
yesterday í gær ee gyairr
youth hostel farfuglaheimili fahrr-fügl-ah-hay-mi-li

Dictionary

ICELANDIC to ENGLISH

a

á eftirlaunum ow ehf-tirr-leörr-nöm retired
á morgun ow morr-gön day after tomorrow (the)
á morgun ow morr-gön tomorrow
aðgangseyrir ath-gowngs-ayrr-irr cover charge
af hverju ahf-kvehrr-yö why
áfengi ow-fayng-yi alcohol
afmæli ahv-mai-li birthday
afsláttur av-slowt-örr discount
akrein ahk-rrayn lane
allt ahlt everything
almenningsþvottahús ahl-mehn-eengs-thvot-ah-hoos launderette
almennt farrými ahl-mehnt fahrr-rreemi economy class
án own without
antík ahn-teek antique
appelsínugul/ur (f/m) ap-ehl-see-nö-gü-lörr orange (colour)
ár owrr year
árstíð owrrs-teeth season

b

bað bahth bath
baðherbergi bahth-hehrr-behrr-gyi bathroom
bær bairr town
bæjarkort baiy-ahrrkorrt map of town
bak bahg back (body)
bakarí bah-ka-rree bakery
bakpoki bahg-pok-yi backpack
bankabók bownk-ah-bohk bank account
banki bownk-yi bank
barn bahdn child
bátur bow-törr boat
beint baynt direct
bensín ben-seen petrol
bensínstöð ben-seen-sterth petrol station

auðkenni eörth-kyehn-i identification
austur eörst-örr east
ávísun ow-vees-ön cheque

biðsalur bith-sahl-ör waiting room
bilað/ur (f/m) bil-ahth/-örr broken/ out of order
bílaleiga bee-lah-laykh-ah car hire
bíll beedl car
bjór byohrr beer
blá/r (f/m) blow/rr blue
blaðasali blahth-ah-sah-li newsagent
bleik/ur (f/m) blayk/-örr pink
bleyja blay-yah diaper/ nappy
blíð/ur (f/m) bleeth/-örr kind
blóðflokkur blohth-flog-örr blood group
bók bohk book
bóka bohk-ah book (make a booking)
bókabúð bohk-ah-booth bookshop
borða borrth-ah eat
borg borrg city
box box box
brátt browt soon
brauð breörth bread
bréf brryehv letter
bremsur brrehms-ör brakes
brjóstahaldari brryohst-ah-hahldah-rr-i bra
bróðir brrohth-irr brother
brottför brrot-ferrr departure
brúðkaupsferðalag brrooth-keörps-ferrth-ah-lahkh honeymoon
brún/n (f/m) brroon/brroodn brown
búð booth booth shop
buxur büx-örr pants/trousers
bygging big-eeng building

d

daglega dahkh-lehkh-ah daily
dagsetning dahkh-seht-neeng date
dagur dahkh-örr day
deila day-lah share
detta deht-ah fall
diskur disk-örr dish
dós dohs can (tin)
dóttir doht-irr daughter
drekka drrehk-ah drink
drykkur drrik-örr drink (beverage)

dýrt deerrt expensive

e

eftirnafn ef-dirrr-nabn surname
eiginkona ay-in-ko-nah wife
eiginmaður ay-yin-mahth-örr husband
einhleyp/ur (f/m) ayn-hlayp/-örr single (person)
einstaklingsherbergi ayn-stahk-leengs-herr-berr-gyi single room
ekkert laust eh-kyerrt leörst no vacancy
elda ehl-dah cook
eldhús ehld-hoos kitchen
ellilífeyrisþegi ehdl-i-leev-ayrr-is-thay-i pensioner
endurgreiðsla ehn-dörr-grrayth-sdla refund
enska ehn-skah English

f

fæðingardagur faith-eeng-ahrr-dahkh-örr date of birth
falleg/ur (f/m) fahdl-ekh/-ör beautiful
fara fah-rrah depart/go/leave
fara að versla fah-rrah ath ves-dla go shopping
fara út fah-rrah go out
farangur far-owng-örr baggage
farangur fahrr-own-görr luggage
farangursband far-owng-örrs-bahnd baggage claim
farangursgeymsla fahrr-own-görrs-gaym-sdlah left luggage (office)
farangursheimild far-owng-örrs-hay-mild baggage allowance
farangursskápar fahrr-own-görrs-skow-pahrr luggage lockers
farði fahrr-thi make-up
farfuglaheimili fahrr-fügl-ah-hay-mi-li youth hostel

fargjald fahrr-gyahld fare
farmiði fahrr-mith-i boarding pass
farsími fahrr-see-mi mobile phone
farþegi fahrr-thay-i passenger
fatageymsla faht-ah-gaym-sdlah
cloakroom
ferð fehrrth tour/trip
ferðaáætlun ferrth-ah-ow-aitl-ön
itinerary
ferðaskrifstofa fehrrth-ah-skrriv-
stov-ah travel agency
ferðataska fehrr-thah-tahs-kah
suitcase
ferðatékki fehrrth-ah-tyehk-yi
travellers cheque
ferja fehrr-yah ferry
ferskt fehrrst fresh
filma (fyrir myndavél) fil-mah (firr-irr
mind-ah-vyehl) film (for camera)
fiskbúð fisk-booth fish shop
fjall fyahdl mountain
fjölskylda fjerl-skild-ah family
flaska flahs-kah bottle
flensa flehn-sah flu
fljót/ur (f/m) flyoht/-örr quick
flóamarkaður floh-ah-mahrrk-ahth-
örr fleamarket
flug flükh flight
flugvallaskattur flükh-vahdl-ah-
skaht-örr airport tax
flugvél flükh-vyehl aeroplane
flugvöllur flükh-verdlörr airport
föt fert clothing
frammistaða frrahm-i-stahth-a
performance
fréttablað frryeht-ah-blath
newspaper
frí frree vacation
frímerki frree-mehrr-kyi stamp
frjálst (óhindrað) frryowlst (oh-hind-
rrahth) free (at liberty)
full/ur (f/m) füdl/-örr drunk
fullbókað füdl-bohk-ahth booked up
fyrirtæki fi-rrirr-tai-kyi company
fyrsta farrými firrst-ah fahrr-rreem-i
first class

g

gallabuxur gahl-ah-büx-örr jeans
ganga gowng-ah walk
garður gahrrth-örr garden
gas gahs gas
gata gah-tah street
gistiheimili gist-i-hay-mi-li
guesthouse
gisting gist-eeng accommodation
gjaldkeri gyahld-kyehrr-i cashier
gjaldkeri gyahld-kyeh-rri teller
gjaldmiðlaskipti gyahld-mith-lah-
skif-ti currency exchange
gjöf gyerv gift
gleraugu glehrr-eörkh-ö glasses
(spectacles)
gluggi glüg-yi window
göngustígur geörng-ö-steekh-örr
footpath
grá/r (f/m) grrow/-rr gray
græn/n (f/m) grrain/grraidn green
grænmeti grrain-meht-i vegetable
gull güdl gold

h

há/r (f/m) how/rr tall
hádegi how-day-i noon
hádegismatur how-day-is-mah-tör
lunch
hæð haith floor (storey)
hætta við hait-ah vith cancel
handklæði hand-klaith-i towel
handverk hahnd-verrk crafts
hanskar hahn-skahr gloves
haust heörst autumn
heimagisting haym-ah-gist-eeng
boarding house
heitt hayt hot
helgidagar hehl-gyi-dahkh-ahrr
vacation (holidays)
helmingur helm-eeng-örr half
herbergi hehrr-behrr-gi room
herbergisnúmer hehrr-behrr-gis-
noom-ehrr room number

hérna hyehd-nah here
hettupeysa heh-tö-pay-sah jumper
hiti hi-ti fever
hjá hyow at
hjálp hyowlp help
hlé hlyeh intermission
hlý/r (f/m) hlee/rr warm
horfa horr-va watch
hósti hohst-i cough
hótel hoh-tehl hotel
hrað (póstur) hrrath (pohst-ör) express (mail)
hraðbanki hrrahht-bown-gyi ATM
hraðbraut hrrath-brreört motorway
hratt hrraht fast
hrein/n (f/m) hrrayn/hrraydn clean
hreinsun hrrayns-ön cleaning
hringja hrreeng-yah call
hundur hünd-örr dog
hvað kvath what
hvar kvahrr where
hvenær kvehnairr when
hver kvehrr each/which/who
hvít/ur (f/m) kveet/ör white

i

í dag ee dahkh today
í fyrradag ee firr-ah-dahkh day before yesterday
í gær ee gyairr yesterday
indælt in-dailt nice
inngangur in-gowng-örr entry
innifalið in-i-fah-lith included
innritun in-rrit-ön check-in (desk)

j

jakki yah-ekki jacket

k

kærasta kairr-ahst-ah girlfriend
kærasti kyairr-ahst-i boyfriend
kaffi kahf-i coffee

kaffihús kahff-i-hoos cafe
kalt kahlt cold
kápa kow-pah coat
karlmaður kahdl-mah-thörr man
kirkja kirr-gyah church
kjóll kyohdl dress
kjörbúð kyerr-booth convenience store
kjöt kyert meat
kjötbúð kyerrt-booth butcher's shop
klink kleenk coins
klukkustund klük-ö-stünd hour
koddaver kod-ah-vehrr pillowcase
koddi kod-i pillow
koma aftur ko-mah af-törr return
komur ko-mör arrivals
kona konah woman
kreditkort krre-dit-korrt credit card
kúl kool cool
kveikjari kvay-gyahrr-i cigarette lighter
kvittun kvit-ön check/receipt
kvöld kverld evening
kvöldmatur kverld-maht-örr dinner

l

læknir laik-nirr doctor
læst laist locked
lág/ur low/lowrr short (height)
landakort lahndahkorrt map of country
landamæri lahn-da-mai-rri border
landpóstur lahn-pohst-örr surface mail (land)
laust leörst vacancy/vacant
lautarferð leört-ahrr-fehrth picnic
leður lehth-örr leather
leið layth path/way
leiðsögn layth-sergn guided tour
leiga lay-kha rent
leigja lay-yah hire
leigubílastopp lay-khö-bee-lah-stop taxi stand
leikrit (leikhús) layk-rrit play (theatre)

leita að layt-ath look for
lestarstöð lehst-ahrr-sterth metro/train station
lín (efni) leen (ehbni) linen (material)
listagallerí list-ah-gahll-ehrr-ee art gallery
loftræsing lofd-rais-eeng air-conditioned
lögreglustöð lerkh-rrehg-lö-sterth police station
lögregluþjónn lerkh-rrehg-lö-thyohdn police officer
lokað lok-ahth closed
lyf liv medicine (medication)
lyfseðill liv-sehth-idl prescription
lyfta lif-tah elevator/ lift
lykill li-kyidl key

m

málaralist mowl-ahrr-ah-list painting (the art)
málari mowl-ahrr-i painter
máltíð mowl-teeth meal
málverk mowl-vehrrk painting (a work)
mamma mahm-ah mother
mánuður mow-nüth-ör month
markaður marrk-ath-ör market
miðasala mi-thah-sah-lah ticket office
miðavél mi-thah-vyehl ticket machine
miðborg mith-borrg city centre
miðdegi mith-day-i midday
miði mi-thi ticket
miði aðra leið mi-thi ahth-rrah layth one-way ticket
miði báðar leiðir mi-thi bow-tharr lay-thirr return (ticket)
miðnætti mith-nait-i midnight
mjólk myohlk milk
morgun morr-gön morning
mótald moh-tahld modem
mótorhjól moh-torr-hyohl motorcycle
myndarleg/ur (f/m) mind-ahrr-lekh/örr handsome
myndavél mind-ah-vyehl camera

n

nærföt nairr-fert underwear
næsti (mánuður) nais-ti (mow-nüth-örr) next (month)
næturklúbbur nait-örr-kloob-örr nightclub
nafn nahbn name
nemi neh-mi student
netkaffi neht-kahf-i Internet cafe
nóg noh enough
norður norrth-ör north
nótt noht night
númer noo-mehrr number
núna noo-nah now

o

ókeypis (gefins) oh-kay-pis (gyeh-vins) free (gratis)
ókunnur maður oh-künn-örr mah-thörr stranger
ökuskírteini erk-ö-skeerr-tayn-i drivers licence
olía o-lee-ah oil
opið op-ith open
opnunartími op-nö-nahrr-tee-mi opening hours
orðabók orrth-ah-bohk dictionary
orðtakabók orth-tahk-ah-bowk phrasebook
öruggt er-ökht safe
óskilamunir oh-skil-ah-mü-nirr lost property office
öskubakki ersk-ü-bahk-i ashtray

p

pabbi pahb-i father
pallur pahdl-örr platform
pappír pahp-eerr paper
partí pahrr-tee party
peningar peh-neeng-ahrr money
peningar til baka peh-neeng-ahrr til bah-kah change (money)
peysa pay-sah sweater

pils pils skirt
plástur plowst-örr Band-Aid
poki pok-yi bag
pósthús pohst-hoos post office
póstkort pohst-korrt postcard
póstnúmer pohst-noo-mehrr post code
póstur pohst-ör mail (postal system)
pund pünd pound (money, weight)
putti püt-i finger

r

rafhlaða rahv-hlahth-ah battery
rán rrown robbery
rauð/ur (f/m) rreörth/-örr red
reiðhjól rrayth-hyohl bicycle
reiðufé rray-thö-fyeh cash
reikning rrayk-neen-görr account
reikningur rrayk-neeng-örr bill
reisa rray-sah journey
reyklaust rrayk-leörst non-smoking
reykur ray-körr smoke
ritfangaverslun rrit-fown-gah-ves-dlön stationer's (shop)
röng (leið) rreörng (layth) wrong (direction)
rúm rroom bed
rúmföt rroom-fert bed linen
rúta rroo-tah bus (intercity)

s

sælkeraverslun sail-kyeh-rrah-ves-dlön delicatessen
sæti sai-ti seat (place)
sætisbelti sai-tis-behl-ti seatbelt
safn sahbn museum
saman sah-mahn together
samband sahm-bahnd connection
seinkun saynk-ön delay
seinna saydn-ah later
seint saynt late
sekt (hegning) sehkht fine (penalty)
sendiráð sehn-di-rrowth embassy
sérhvert syehrr-kvehrrt every

servíetta sehrr-vee-yeht-ah napkin
setustofa seht-u-stov-ah transit lounge
síðasta seeth-ahst-ah last (previous)
síðdegi seeth-day-yi afternoon
silfur sil-vörr silver
silki sil-kyi silk
símaklefi seem-ah-kleh-vi phone box
símaskrá seem-ah-skrow phone book
símkort seem-korrt phone card
sjálfsafgreiðsla sjowls-ahv-grayth-sdla self service
sjópóstur sjoh-pohst-örr surface mail (sea)
sjór syoh-rr sea
sjúkrahús syook-rrah-hoos hospital
skartgripir skahrrt-grri-pirr jewellery
skíðalyfta skee-tha-lift-ah chairlift (skiing)
skilríki skil-rreekyi identification card (ID)
skipta skif-tah exchange
skiptimynt skif-ti-mint change (coins)
skítugt skee-tökht dirty
skjalataska skyah-lah-tahsk-ah briefcase
skógur skohkh-örr forest
skór skohrr shoe
skráningarskírteini skrrow-neeng-ahrr-skeerr-tay-ni car registration
skrifstofa skrriv-sto-vah office
skyggna skig-nah slide (film)
skyrta skirrtah shirt
smábarn smow-bahdn baby
smokkur smok-örr condom
snarl snahrrdl snack
snemma sdnehmm-ah early
snjór snyohrr snow
snyrtistofa snirr-di-stov-ah beauty salon
sokkabuxur sok-ah-bux-örr pantyhose
sokkar sok-ahrr socks
sonur son-örr son
staðfesta stahth-fehst-ah validate
staðfesta (bókun) stahth-fehst-ah (bohk-ön) confirm (a booking)

stærð stairrth size (general)
stefnumót sdehb-nü-moht appointment
stelpa stehl-pah girl
stigi stee-yi stairway
stolið sto-lith stolen
stoppistöð stop-i-sterr-th bus stop
stór stohrr big
stórmarkaður stohrr-mahrk-ahth-örr supermarket
stórt stohrrt large
stórverslun stohrr-ves-dlön department store
strætó strrai-toh bus (city)
strákur strrow-körr boy
strönd strernd beach
sturta stürr-tah shower
suður sü-thörr south
sumar sü-mahrr summer
sundlaug sund-leörkh swimming pool
svefnherbergi svehb-hehrr-behrr-gyi bedroom
svefnpoki svehb-po-gyi sleeping bag
svefnvagn svehb-vahgn sleeping car
sveitin svay-tin countryside
svört/svartur (f/m) svehrrt/svahrrt-örr black
synda sind-ah swim
sýning see-neeng exhibition/show
systir sis-tirr sister

t

teppi teh-bi blanket
texti tehx-ti subtitles
til til to
til baka til bah-kah change
tímaáætlun tee-mah-ow-ait-lön timetable
tími tee-mi time
tíska teesk-ah fashion
tollur todl-örr customs
tölva terl-vah computer
tónlistarbúð tohn-list-ahrr-booth music shop
torg torrg square (town)

trygging trrig-eeng deposit
tryggingar trrig-eeng-ahrr insurance
túlkur toolk-ör interpreter
tvíbreitt rúm tvee-brrayt rroom double bed
tvö rúm tver rroom twin beds
tvöfalt herbergi tver-fahlt hehrr-behrr-gyi double room
týnd/ur (f/m) teend/-örr lost

u

ull üdl wool
umferðarmiðstöð üm-ferrth-ahrr-mith-sterth bus station
umfram (farangur) üm-frrahm (fahrr-owng-ör) excess (baggage)
umslag üm-sdlag envelope
upphitað üp-hit-ahth heated
upplýsingamiðstöð üp-lees-eeng-ah-mith-sterth tourist office
upplýsingar üp-lees-eeng-ahrr information
upptekin/n (f/m) üp-tehk-yin busy
út á lífið oot ow lee-vith night out
útgangur oot-gowng-ör exit
útlensk/ur (f/m) ootlehnsk/-örr foreign
útsýni oot-seen-i view

v

vasahnífur vah-sah-hnee-vörr penknife
vatn vahthn water
vegabréf vehkh-ah-brryehf passport
vegabréfsnúmer vehkh-ah-brryehfs-noom-ehrr passport number
vegur vehkh-ör road/route
veik/ur (f/m) vayk/-örr ill/sick
veitingavagn vay-teeng-ah-vahgn dining car
vekjaraklukka veh-gyah-rrah-klük-ah alarm clock
verð vehrrth price
verslun ves-dlön grocery

verslunarmiðstöð ves-dlön-ahrr-mith-sterth shopping centre
vestur vest-örr west
vetur veh-törr winter
viðgerð vith-gyehrth repair
viðskiptafarrými vith-skift-ah-fahrr-rree-mi business class
viðskipti vith-skift-i business
viðstödd/staddur (f/m) vith-sterd present
vika vi-kah week
vín veen wine
vinur vin-örr friend
vont vont bad
vor vorr spring (season)

w

wifi vai-fai wifi

y

yfirmaður i-virr-mah-thörr manager (restaurant, hotel)

þ

þægilegt thai-yi-lekht comfortable
þakklát/ur (f/m) thahk-low-törr grateful
þjóðvegur thyohth-vehkh-örr highway
þjónusta thyoh-nūs-tah service
þjónustugjöld thyoh-nūs-tu-gyerld service charge
þjórfé thyohrr-fyeh tip (gratuity)
þrífa three-vah wash (something)
þurrt thürrt dry
þvottavél thvot-ah-vyehl washing machine
þvottur thvot-örr laundry (clothes)

Acknowledgments

Associate Product Director Angela Tinson

Product Editor Sandie Kestell

Language Writers Gunnlaugur Bjarnason, Ingibjörg Árnadóttir, Margrét Eggertsdóttir

Cover Designer Campbell McKenzie

Cover Researcher Wibowo Rusli

Thanks

Kate Chapman, Gwen Cotter, James Hardy, Indra Kilfoyle, Elizabeth Jones, Juan Winata

Published by Lonely Planet Global Ltd
CRN 554153

1st Edition – June 2018
Text © Lonely Planet 2018
Cover Image Hikers under the northern lights, powerofforever/Getty Images©

Printed in China 10 9 8 7 6 5 4 3 2 1

Contact lonelyplanet.com/contact

MIX
Paper from
responsible sources
FSC™ C021741
www.fsc.org

Index

10. Phrases to Get You Talking

Hello.	Halló. hahl-loh
Goodbye.	Bless. blehs
Please.	Gjörðu svo vel. gyer-thö svo vehl
Thank you.	Takk fyrir. tahk firr-irr
Excuse me (forgive me).	Afsakið. ahf-sahk-ith
Sorry.	Mér þykir það leitt. myehrr <u>th</u>i-kirr <u>th</u>ahth layht
Yes.	Já. yow
No.	Nei. nay
I don't understand.	Ég skil (ekki). yehkh skil (ehk-i)
How much is it?	Hvað kostar þetta? kvahth kos-dahrr theth-ah